I0491587

OrnaMENTALs Lights Out

A SuziQ Creations Publication

More Coloring Books by Sue Chastain

OrnaMENTALs Whimsical Mandalas

OrnaMENTALs Splendid Symmetry

MiniMENTALs On-the-Go Coloring Book

OrnaMENTALs Feel Good Words

OrnaMENTALs Feel Good Words To-Go

Available from Amazon.com.
Digital versions and single pages available from suziqcreations.com for instant download.

Praise for OrnaMENTALs

" Very enjoyable book. I love the positivity of it in this negative world. The artistry of the pictures is superb. I would recommend for anyone! " – M. Whitworth

"...the designs are so well executed, the lines are clean and the variety is great! From cute, whimsical images like the frog, to mandalas, to patterns, to flowers, I never know what's going to be next!" – Ali

"Finding your site has brought such a HUGE smile to my face. Your designs are absolutely awesome. Your creativity has inspired me to try new things." – Crie

"This is exactly the style of coloring pages that I like. Some detail, but not so detailed that I lose patience/interest. These are fun sized pages that you can easily finish in an evening." – Roseanne

"A little-sized book with a lot of big things going for it!" - John

"Working in a noisy sometimes hectic environment can leave you stressed. These coloring pages can be a great, quiet, time relaxer. There is a nice collection of art to color in this book from simple to more complex, limited only by your imagination." - David

"Beautiful book, full of amazing designs. I can't believe how intricate each page is, and how fun to color. Adults need something like this to relax, de-stress, and rewire their brains." - Mae

"There are so many different designs to choose from, it is impossible to get bored with this book!" - Jessica

"So uplifting, encouraging and delightful to color - I have already recommended it to multiple friends. EVERYONE needs encouragement and positive affirmation in their life, and this book does that and more!" - G. Albert

OrnaMENTALS™

COLORING FUN FOR ALL AGES

LIGHTS OUT

LIGHTHEARTED DESIGNS TO COLOR WITH DRAMATIC BLACK BACKGROUNDS

BY SUE CHASTAIN

ORNAMENTALS™ LIGHTS OUT COLORING BOOK
Copyright © 2016 by Sue Chastain. All rights reserved.
SuziQCreations.com

Cover and Book Design by Sue Chastain

ISBN-13: 978-1-945691-01-0
ISBN-10: 1-945691-01-8

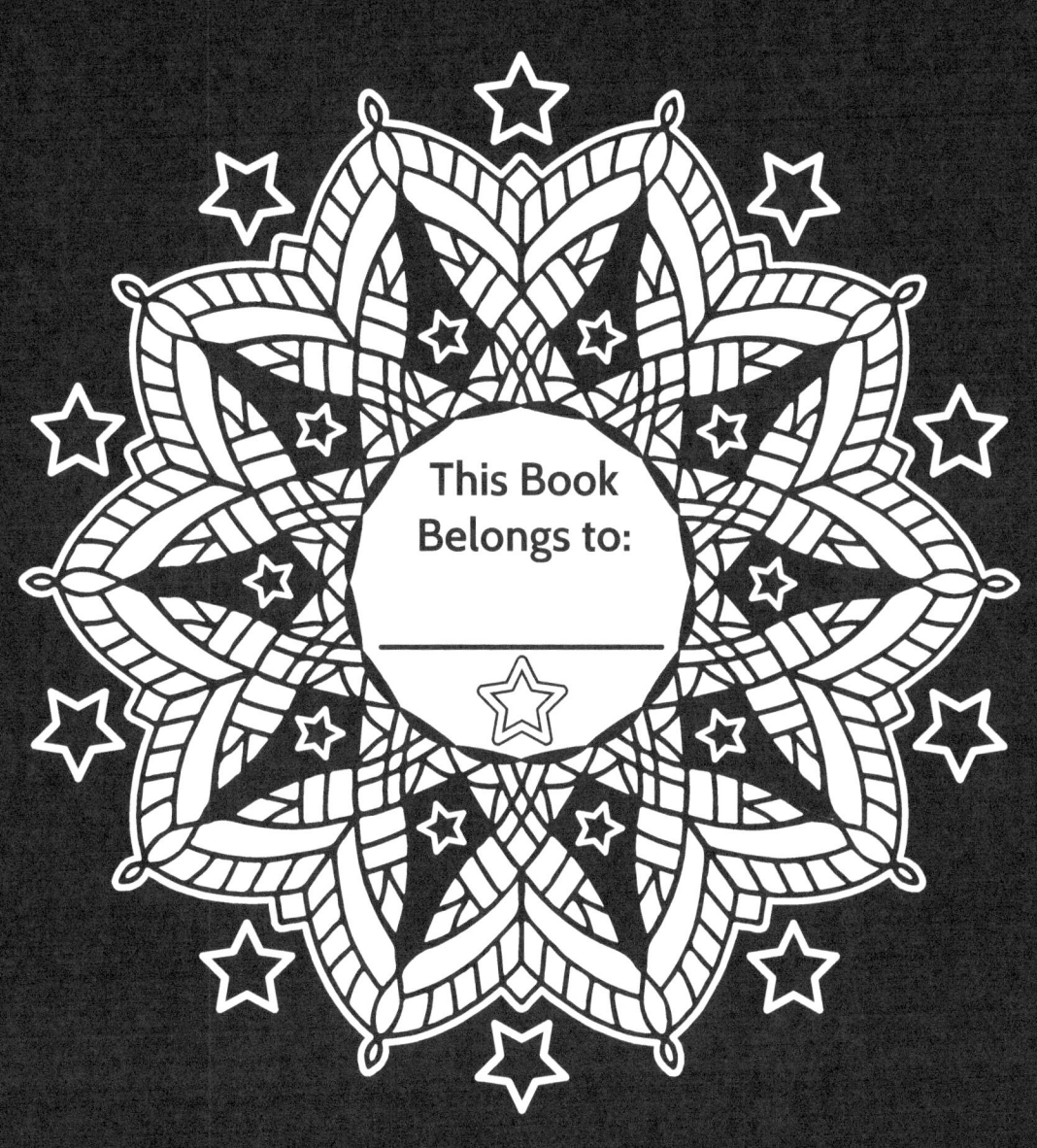

This Book
Belongs to:

_____

A NOTE FROM THE ARTIST...

Thank you so much for choosing this book! It's hard to believe that less than one short year after publishing my first coloring book, I'm writing this introduction for the sixth OrnaMENTALs™ coloring book.

I am awed and deeply thankful to all the fans who have purchased my books and brought their amazing talent and creative vision to my designs. Thank you for helping me live my dream. I especially want to thank my dear husband for giving me the freedom to take the leap and try this "being an artist" thing, and for putting up with the wacky mood swings of a ~~crazy~~ creative person. Thanks also to my family for encouraging me throughout this journey. Last, and definitely not least, I am so grateful to my incredible and talented team—you know who you are.

So here it is. Book number six. *OrnaMENTALs Lights Out* consists of 40 lighthearted illustrations with dramatic black backgrounds and accents that will make your coloring come to life in new and exciting ways. All the designs are original creations. Some are remixed favorites from previous books, but most were created specifically for black backgrounds and have never been previously published. This book has been so fun to make and I hope you enjoy coloring it as much as I enjoyed making it.

The illustrations in this book range in difficulty from simple to moderately intricate and are suitable for all ages and coloring skill levels. The book can be colored with colored pencils, markers, gel pens, even crayons. Images are printed on only one side of the paper to mitigate bleed-through, but if you use markers or pens, I suggest putting a blank sheet of paper behind the design you are coloring. You will find several pages in the back of the book which you can tear out to use for this purpose. If you wish to use very wet media such as watercolors, you'll want to copy the pages onto heavier paper such as card stock. Making copies for personal use to color multiple times is permitted.

At the back of the book you will find some color test sheets and bonus pages (samples from my other books), plus useful links. Be sure to visit the website and sign up for my value-packed newsletter, *Sue's News*!

Get ready to see your creative exploration come to life in vivid color with the added drama of black backgrounds. Now cozy up with your favorite coloring tools and have fun with *Lights Out*.

Stay in touch and happy coloring,

Sue Chastain
suziqcreations.com

PS: If you enjoy this book, please review it on Amazon.

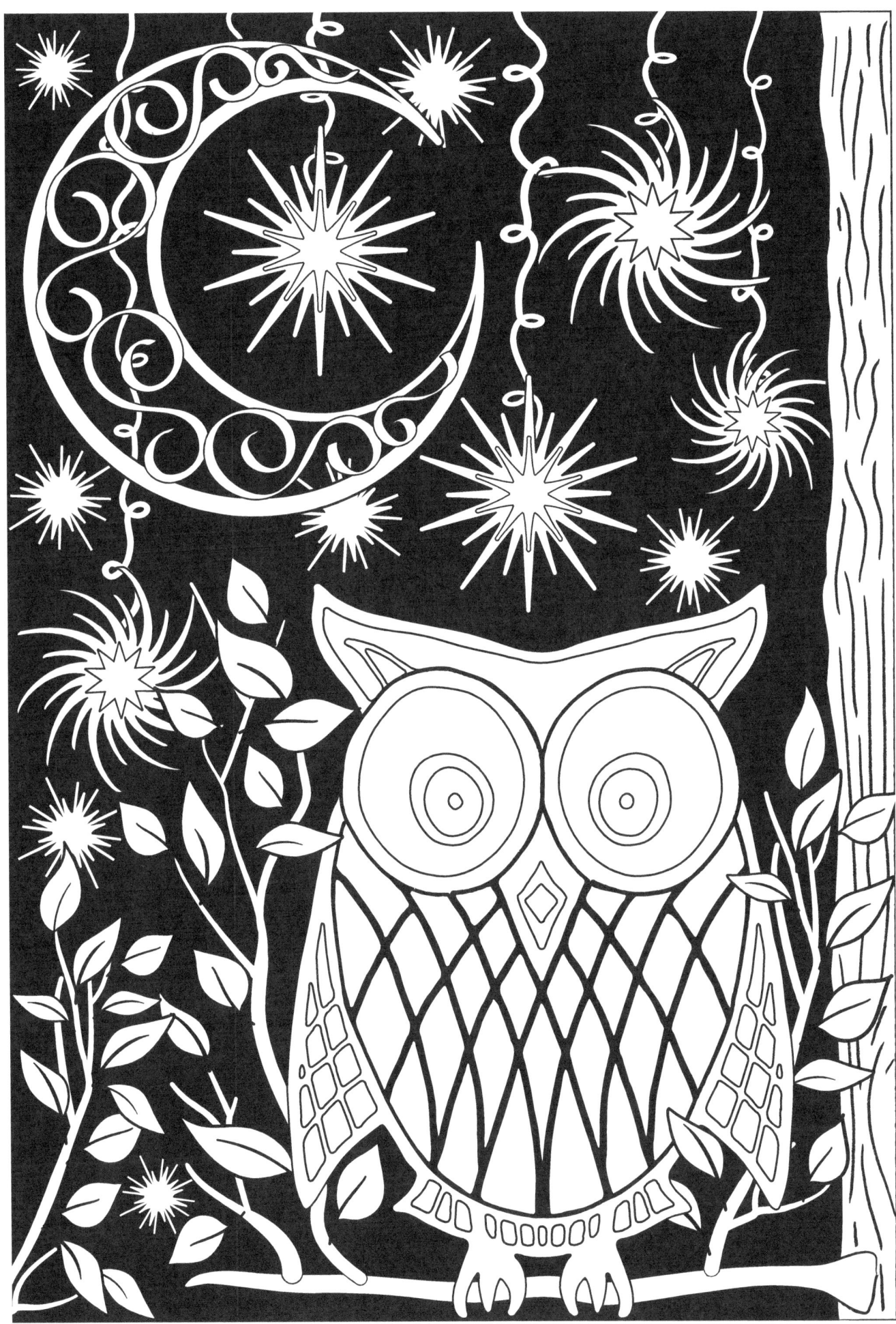

Colored by: _____

OrnaMENTALs™ #0043 remix "Dragonflies Dance at Midnight"   Colored by: _____

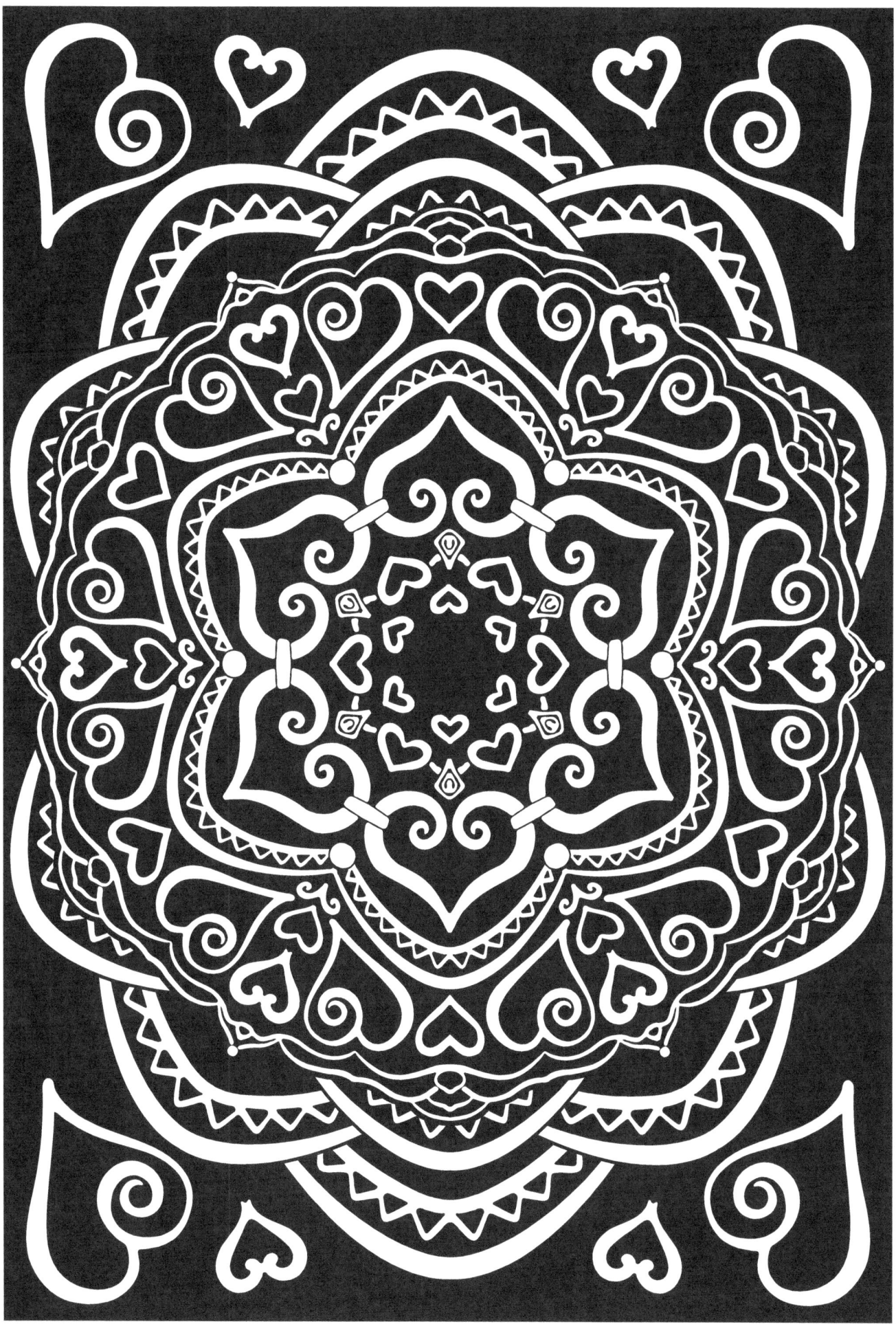

Colored by: _____

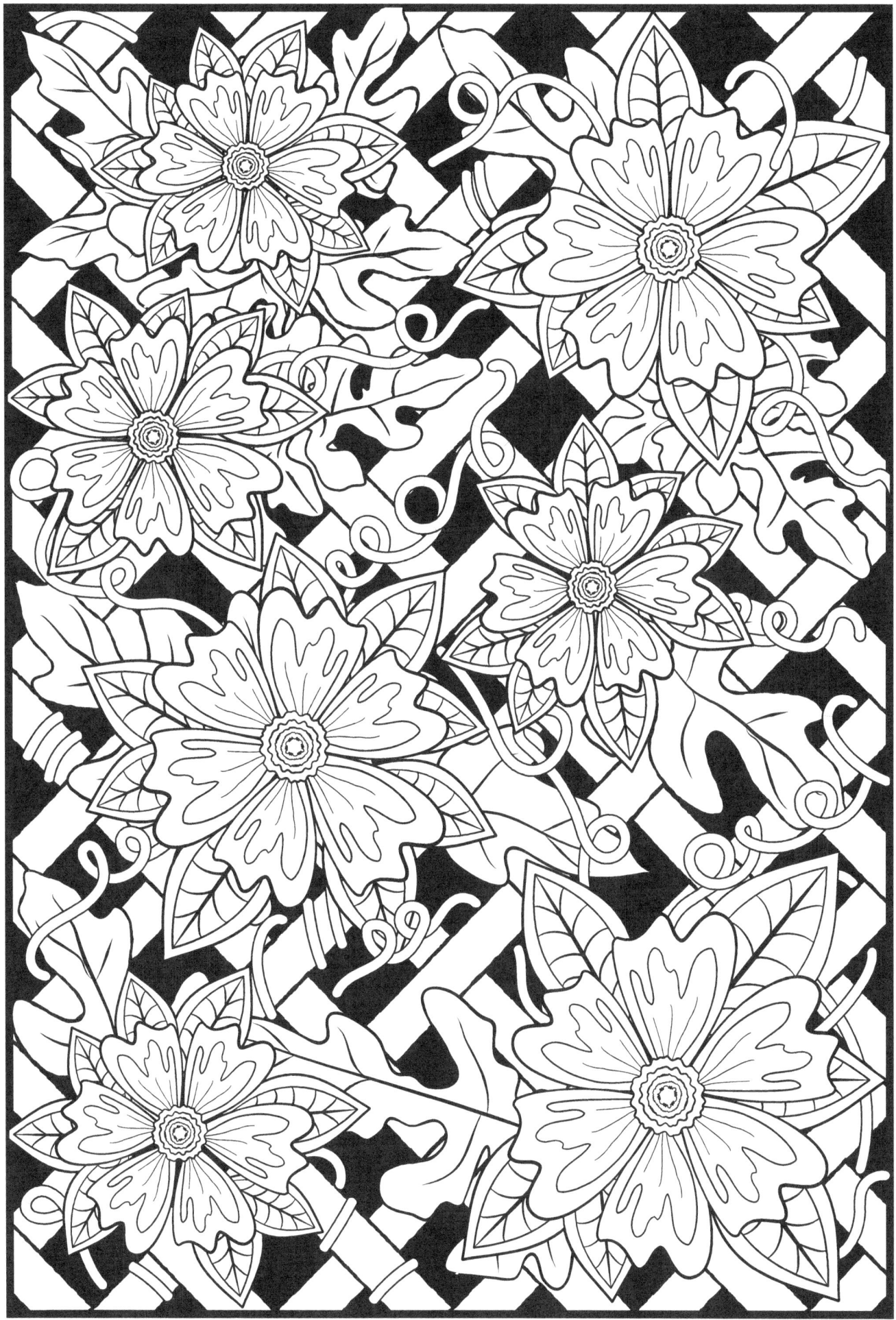

Colored by: _____

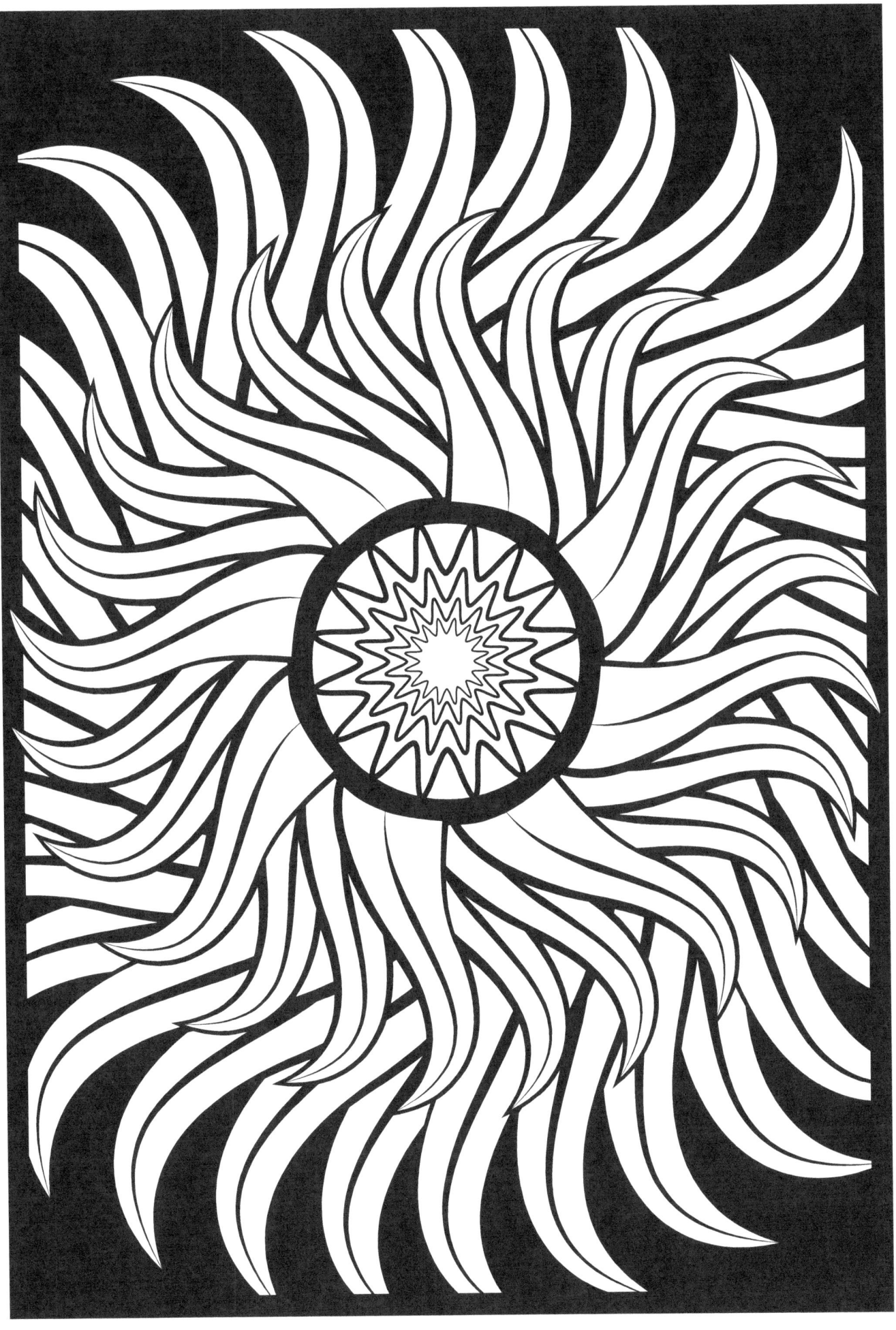

Colored by: _____

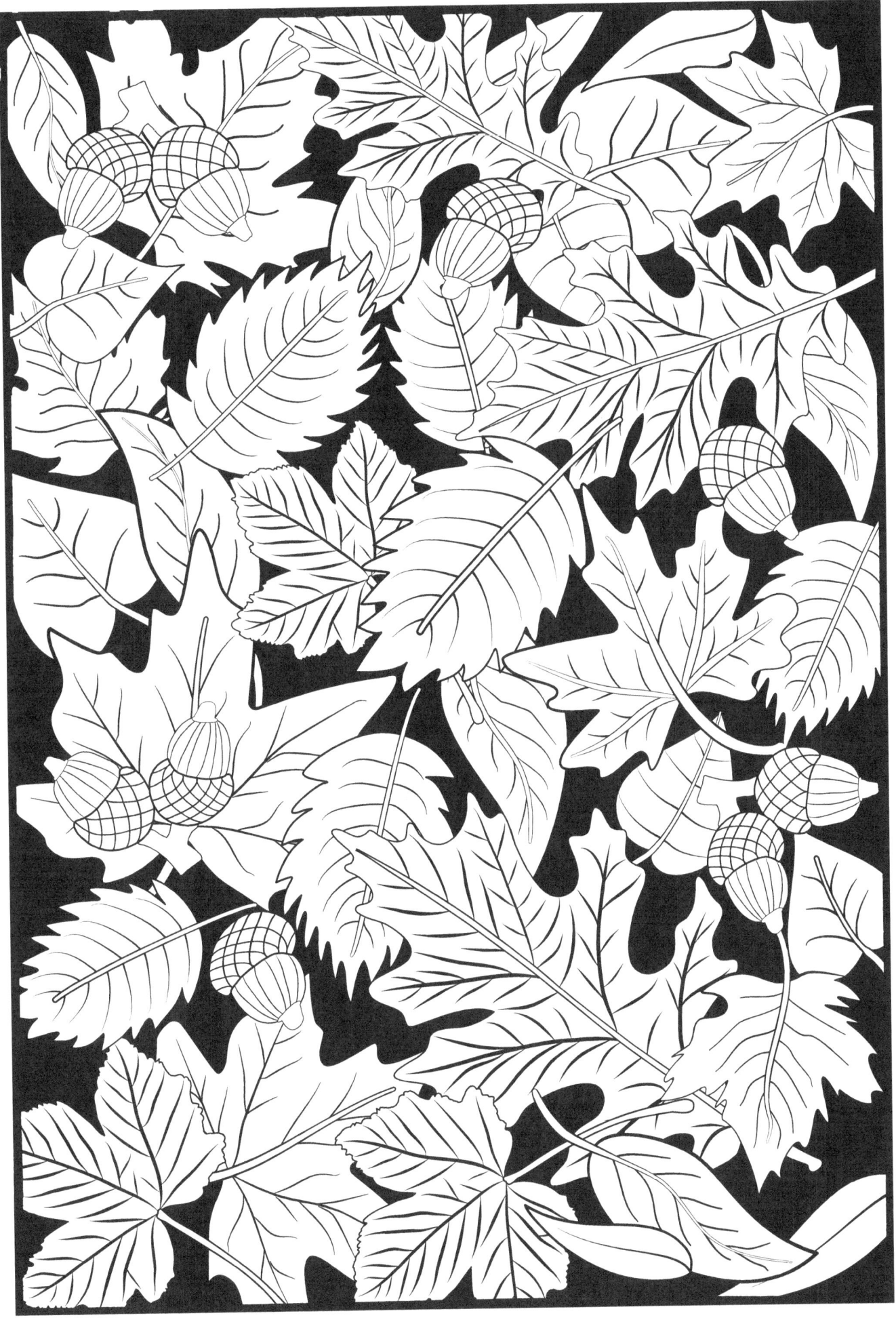

Colored by: _____

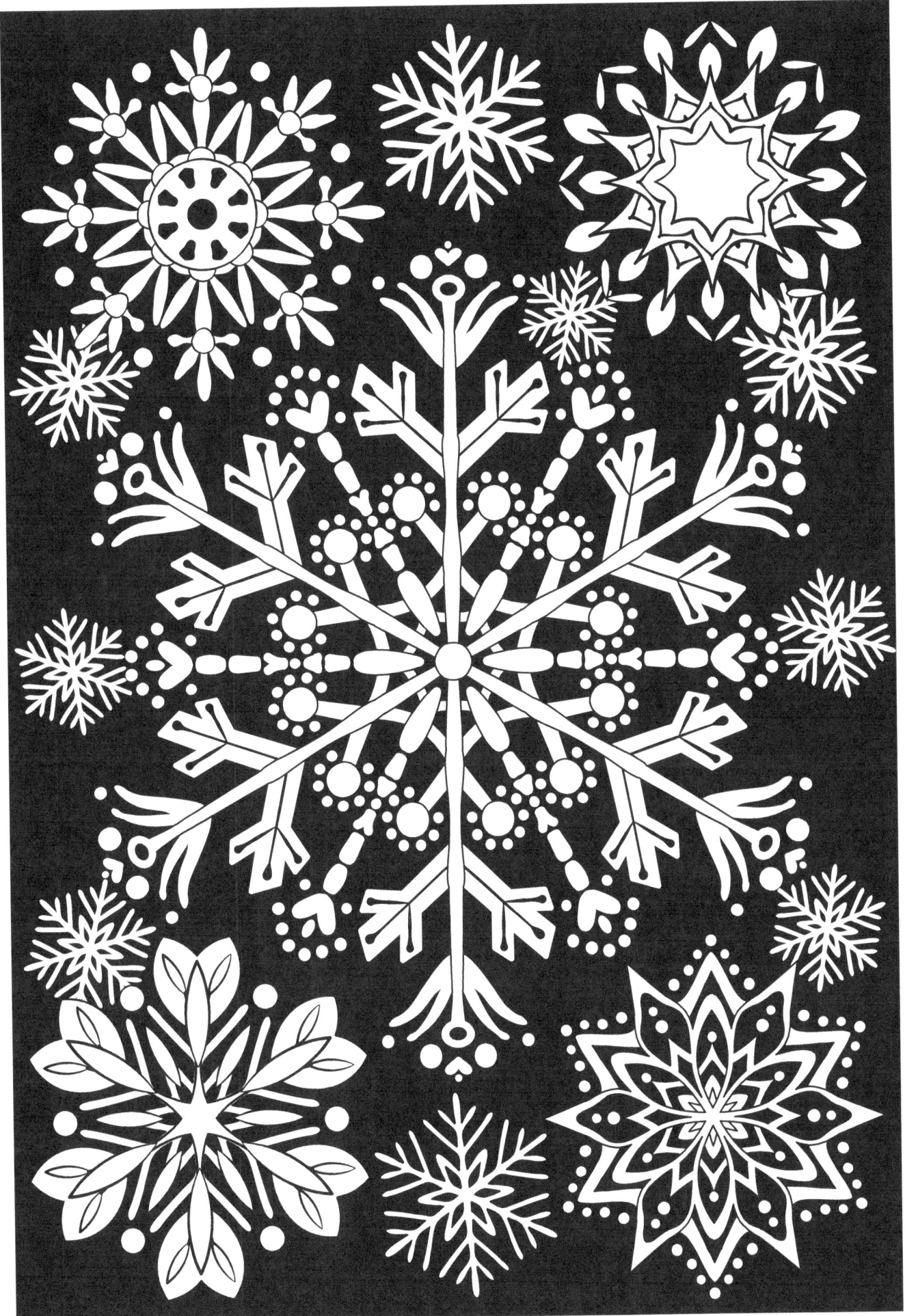

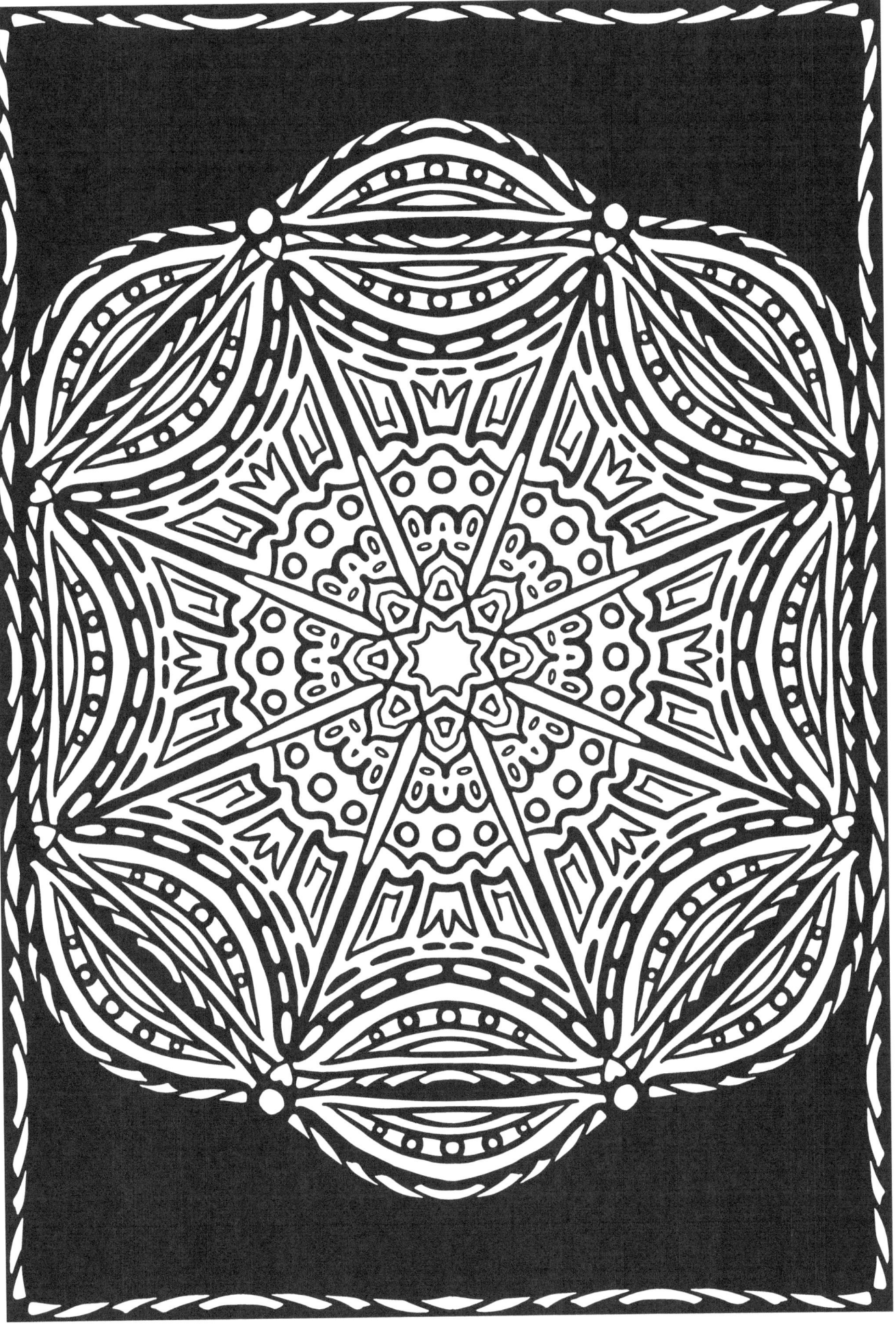

Colored by: _____

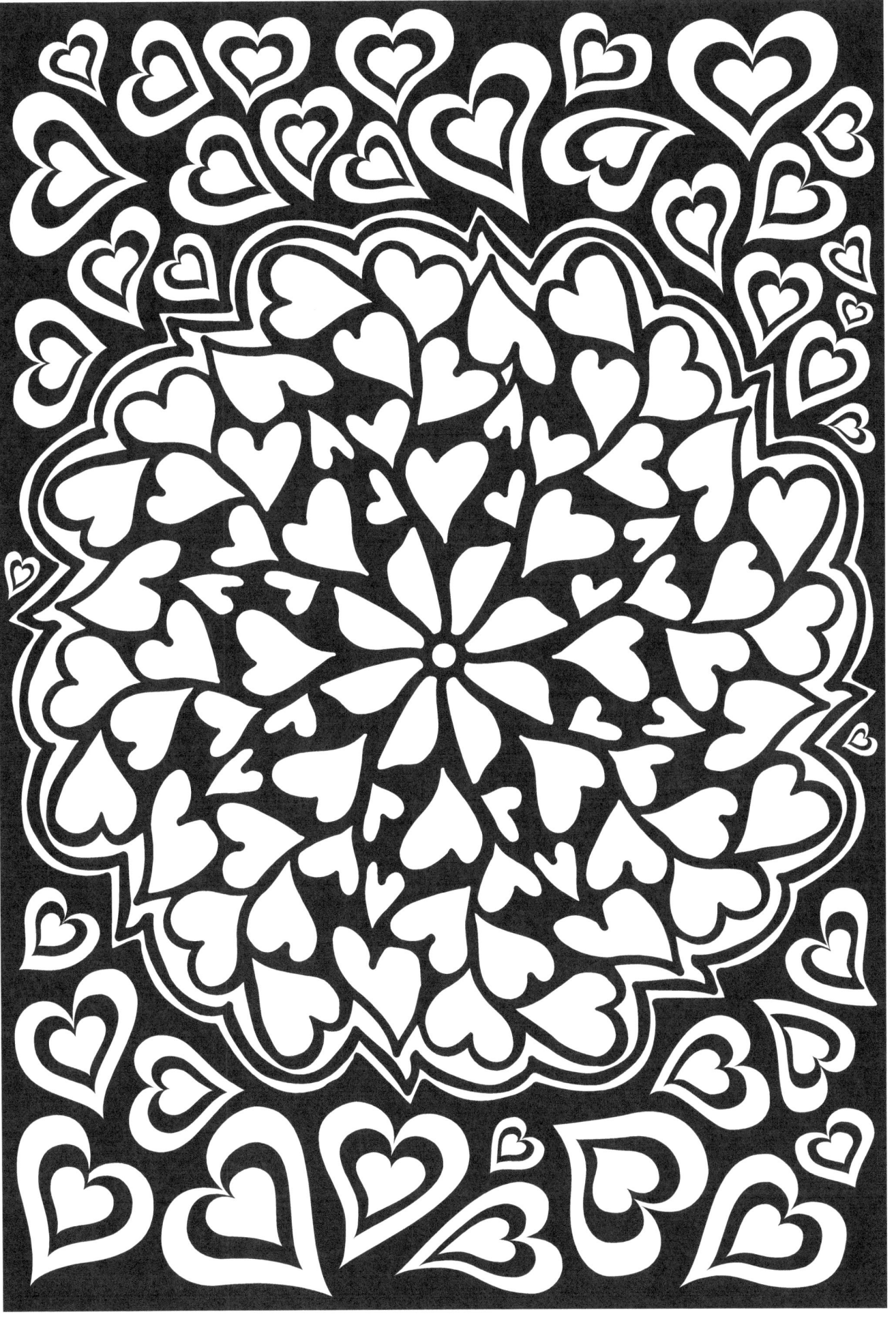

Colored by: _____

Colored by: _____

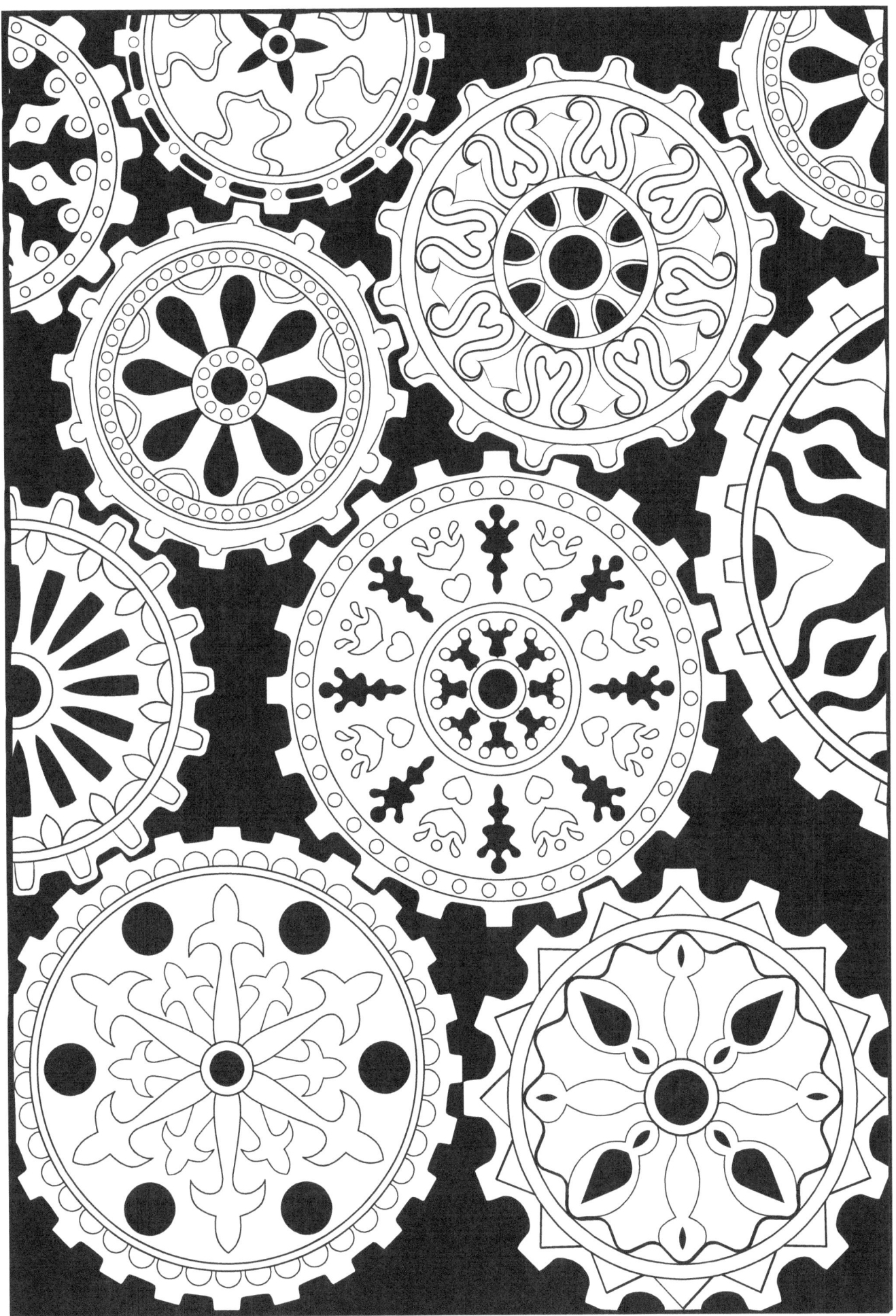

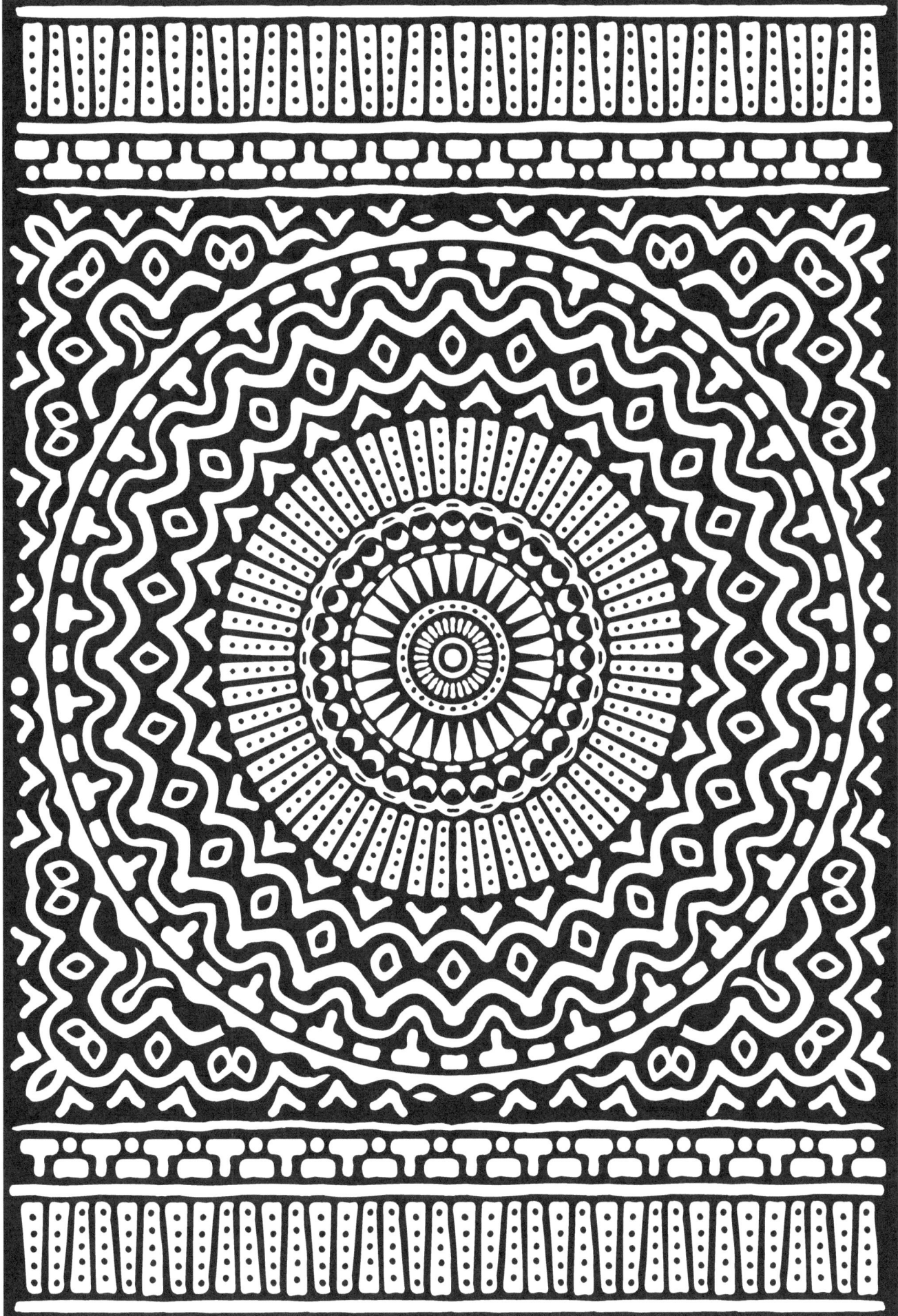

Colored by: _____

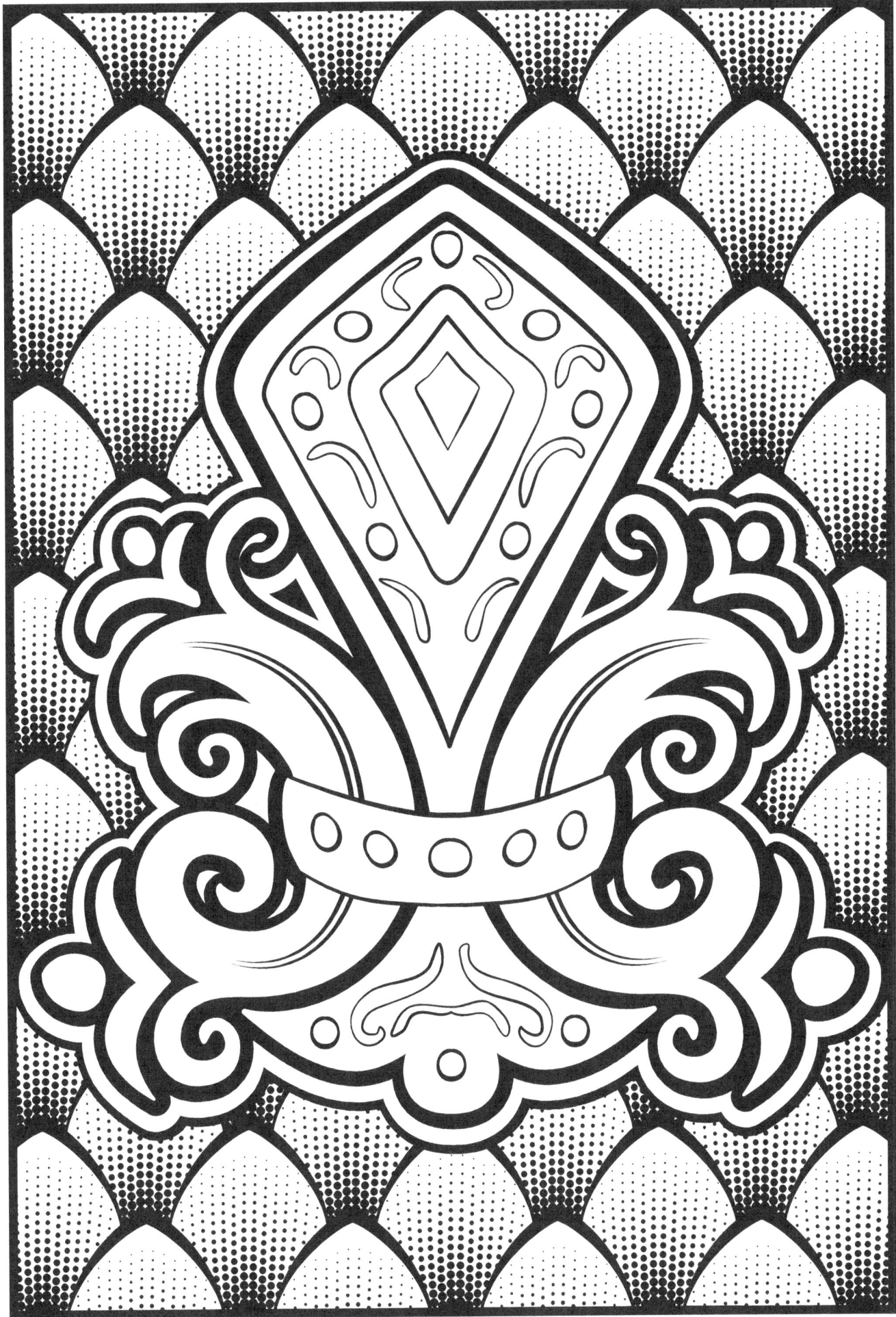

Colored by: _____

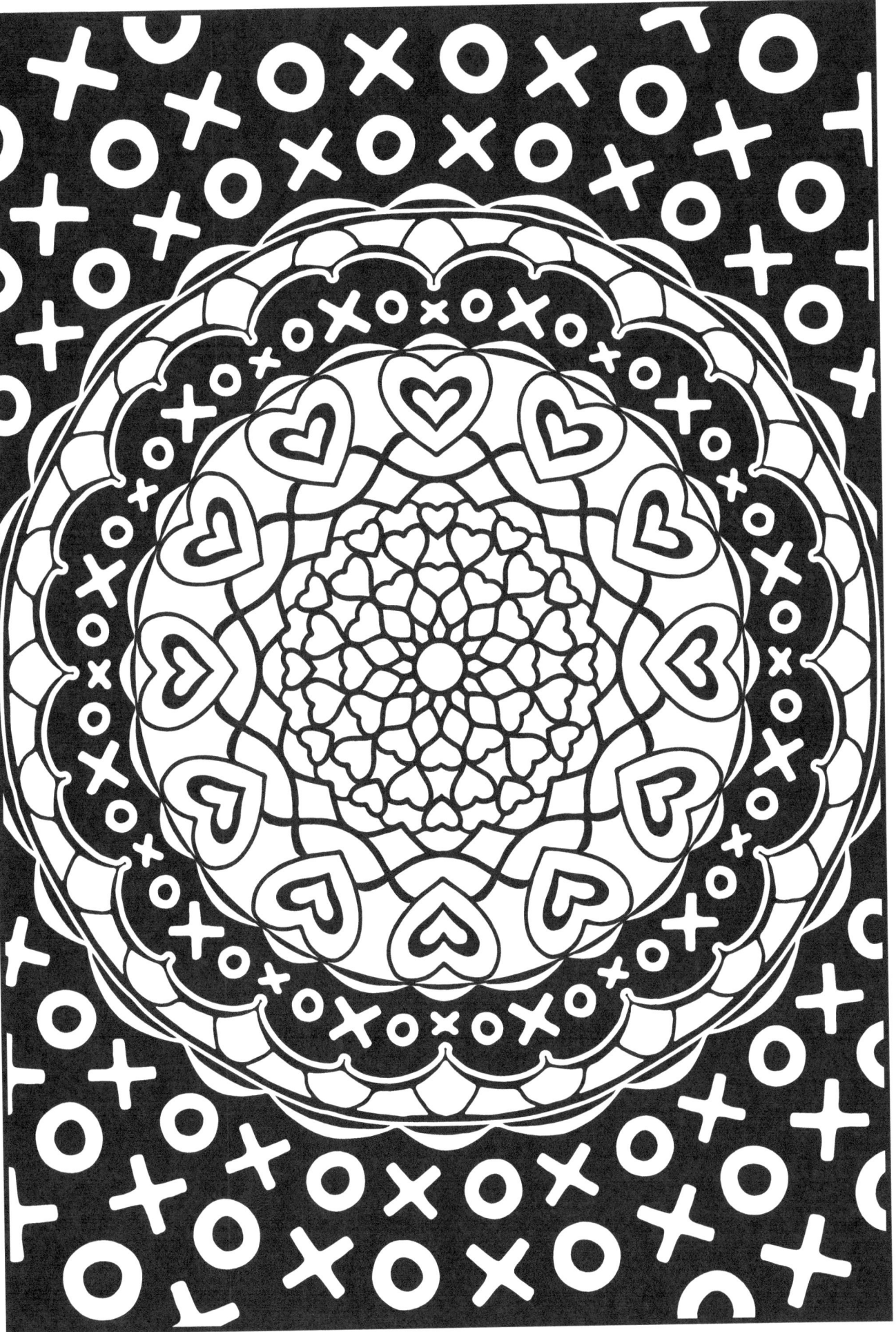

Colored by: _____

Colored by: _____

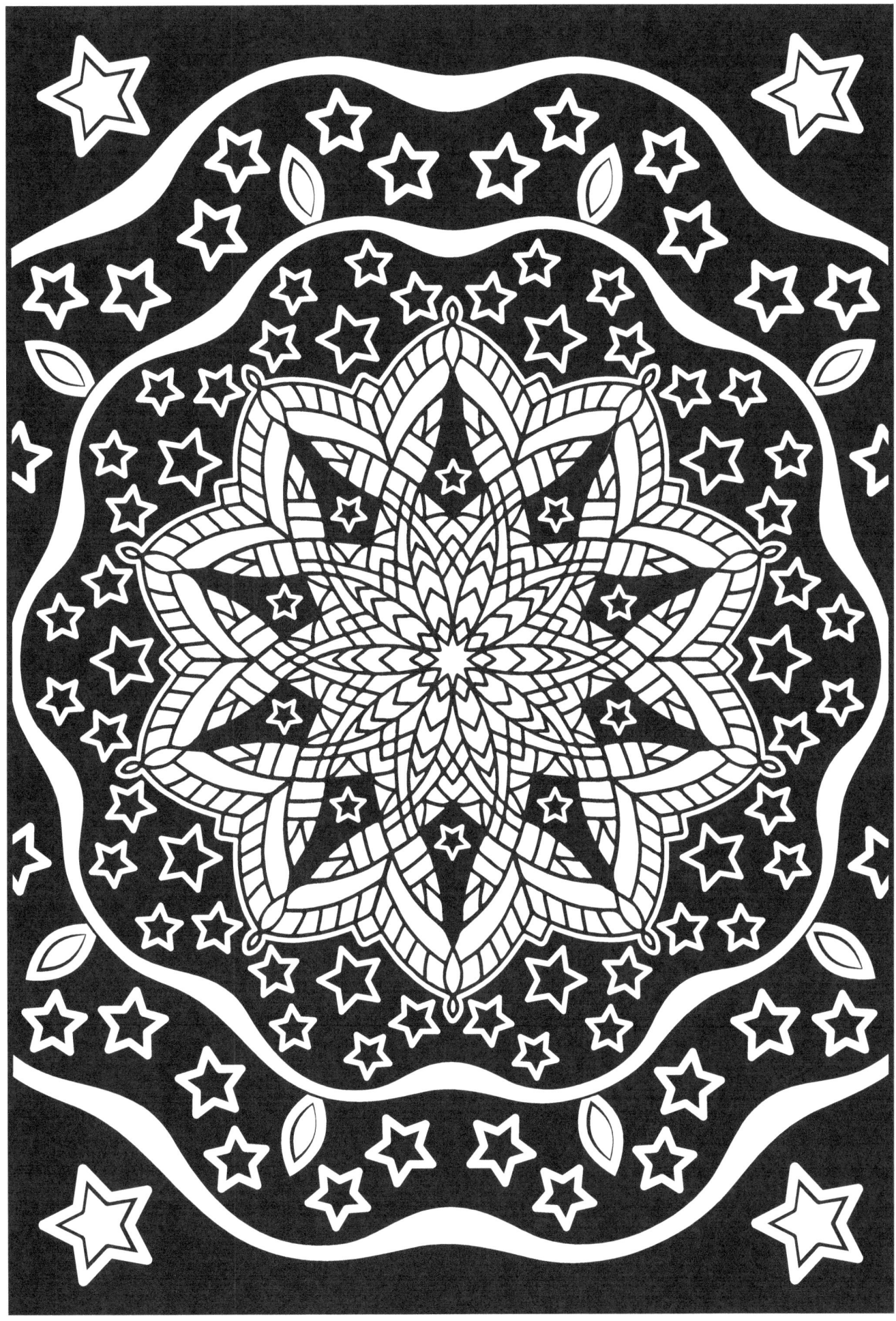

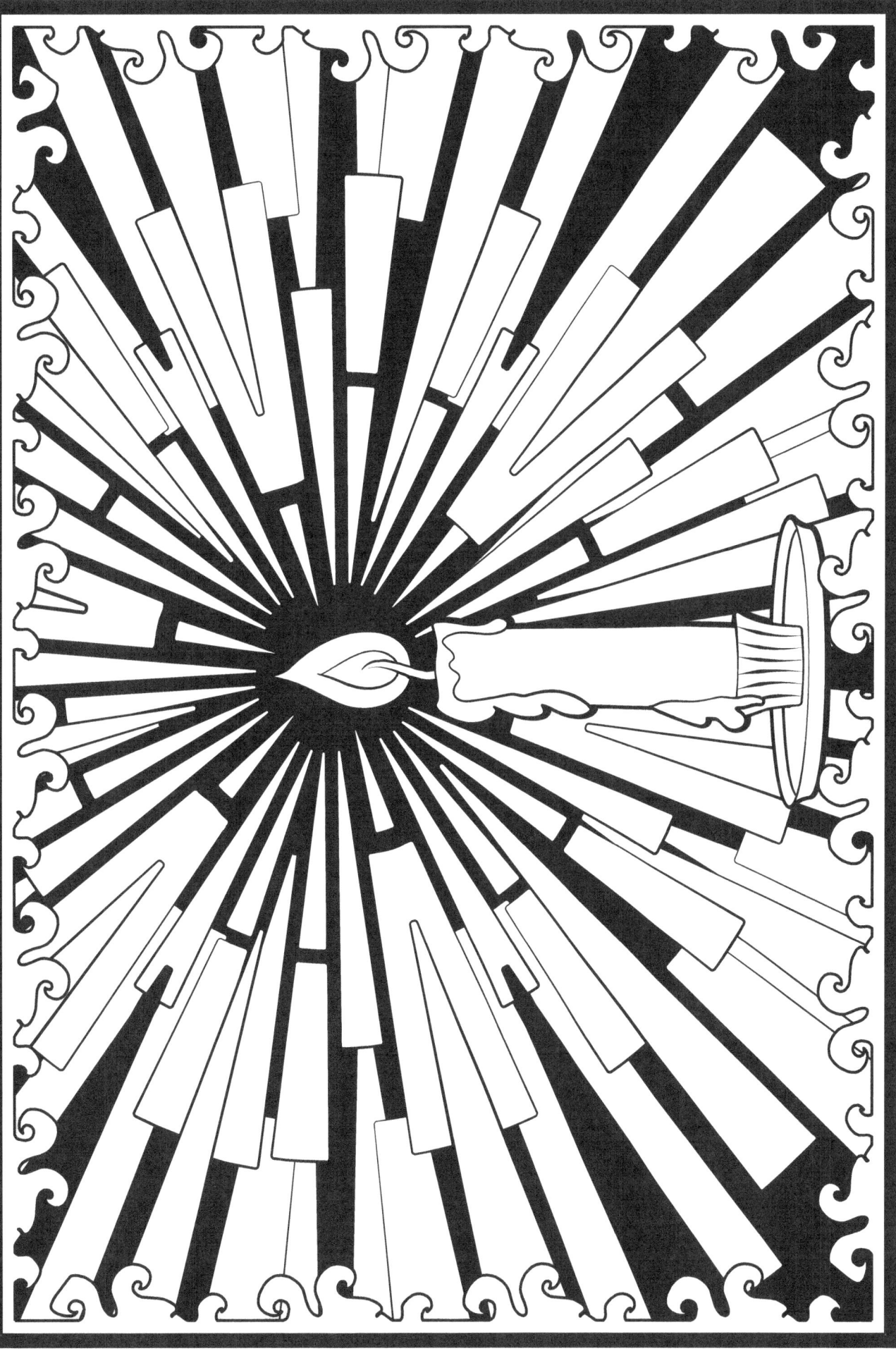

Colored by: _____

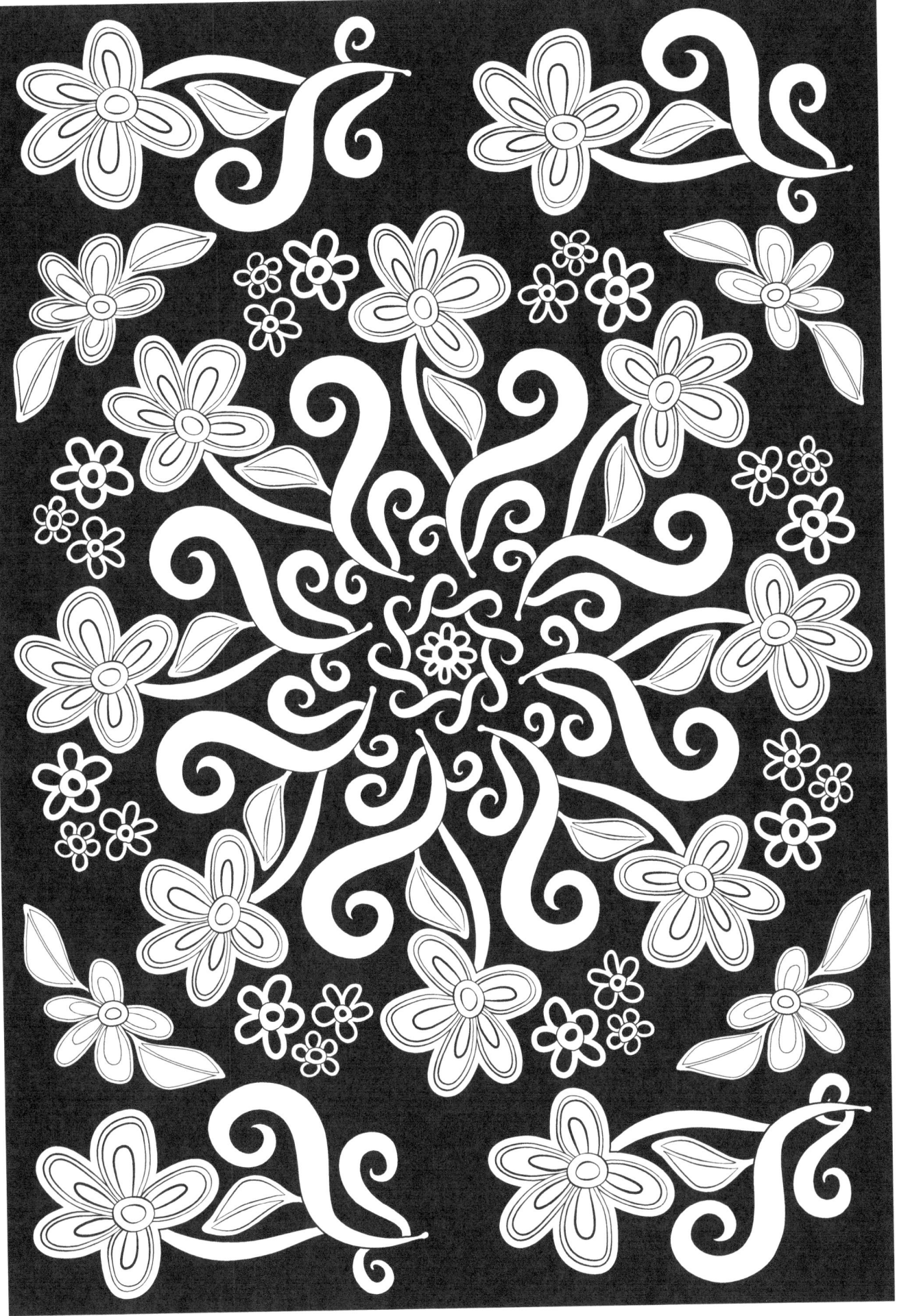

Colored by: _____

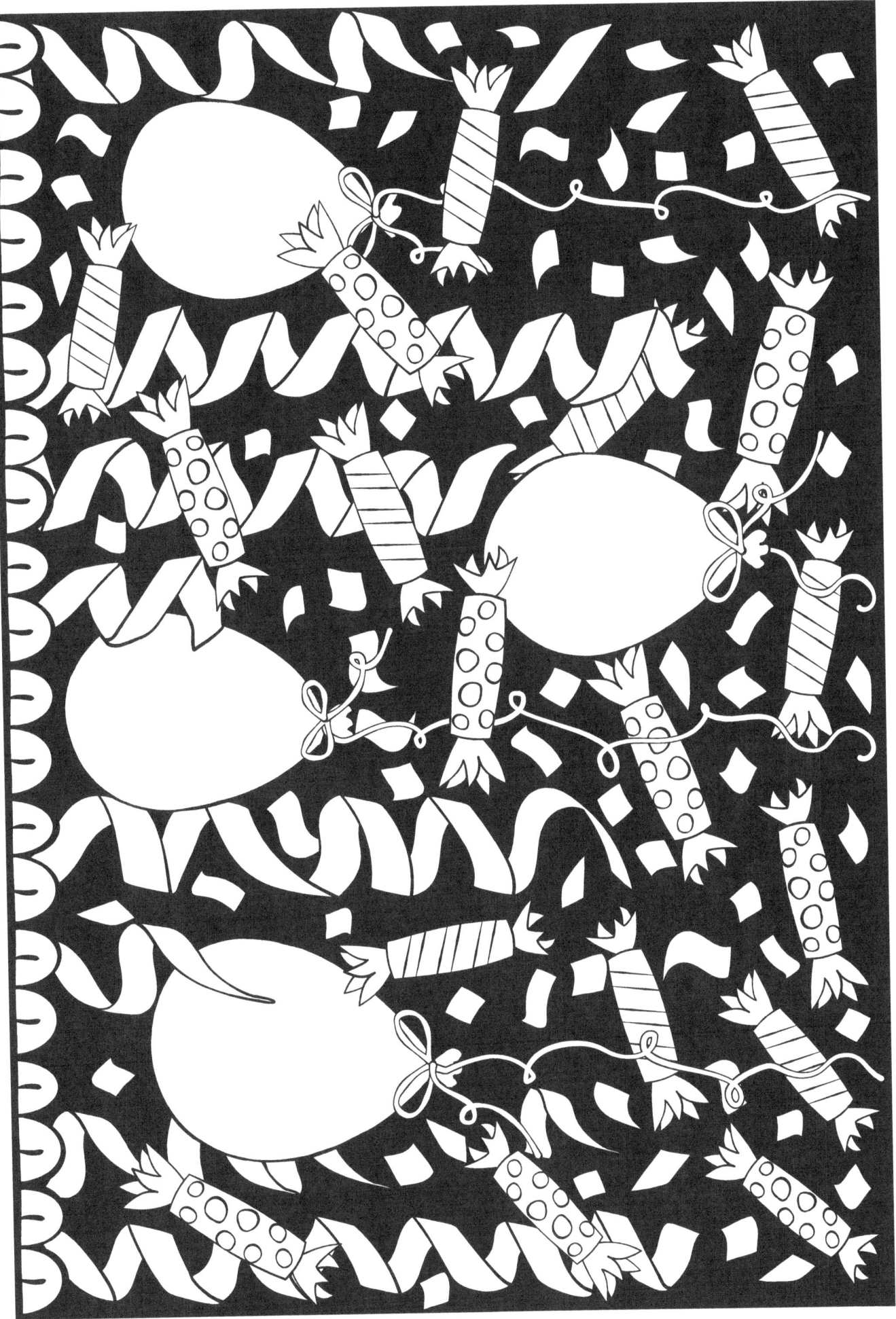

Colored by: _____

OrnaMENTALs™ #0112 "Celebration"

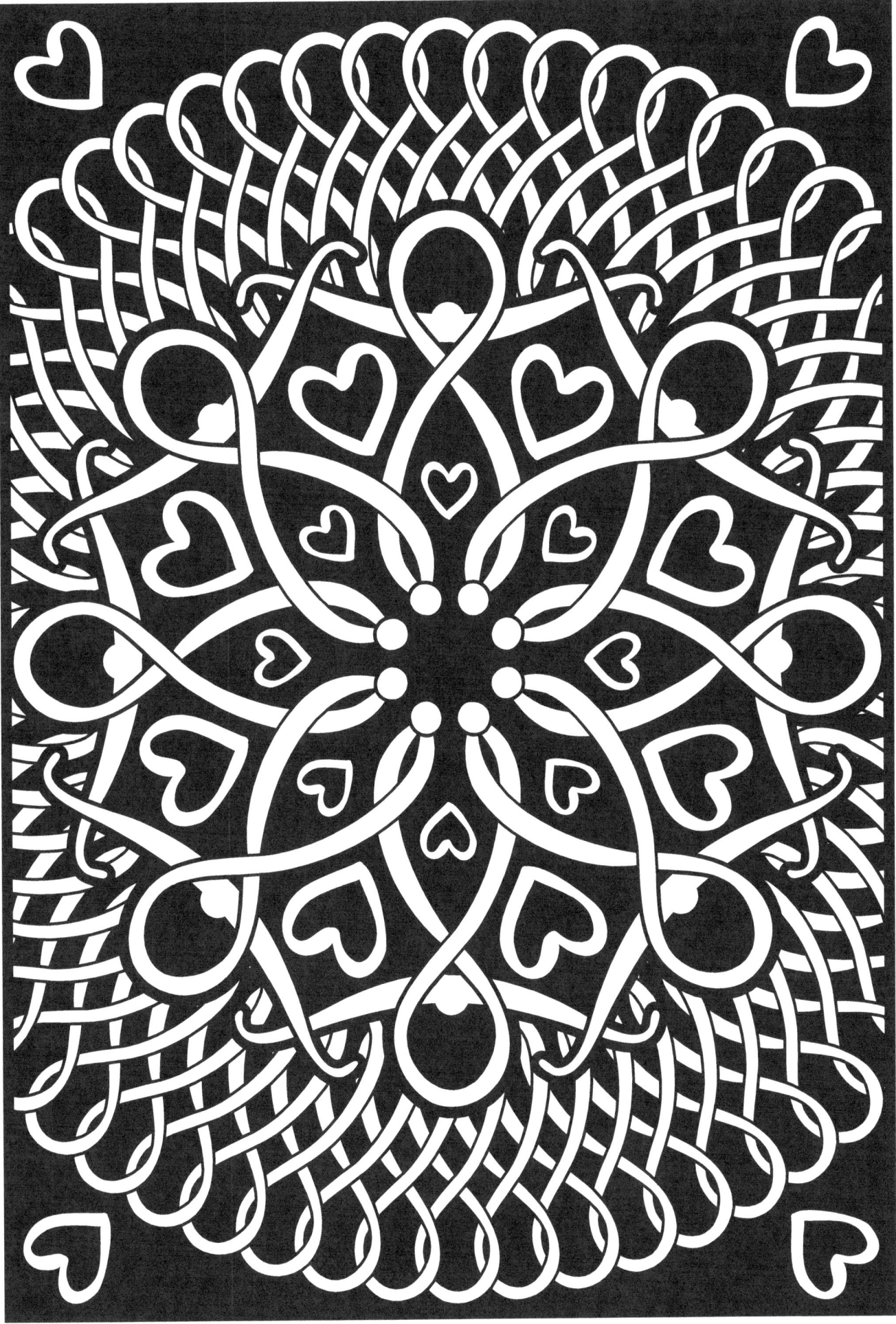

Colored by: _____

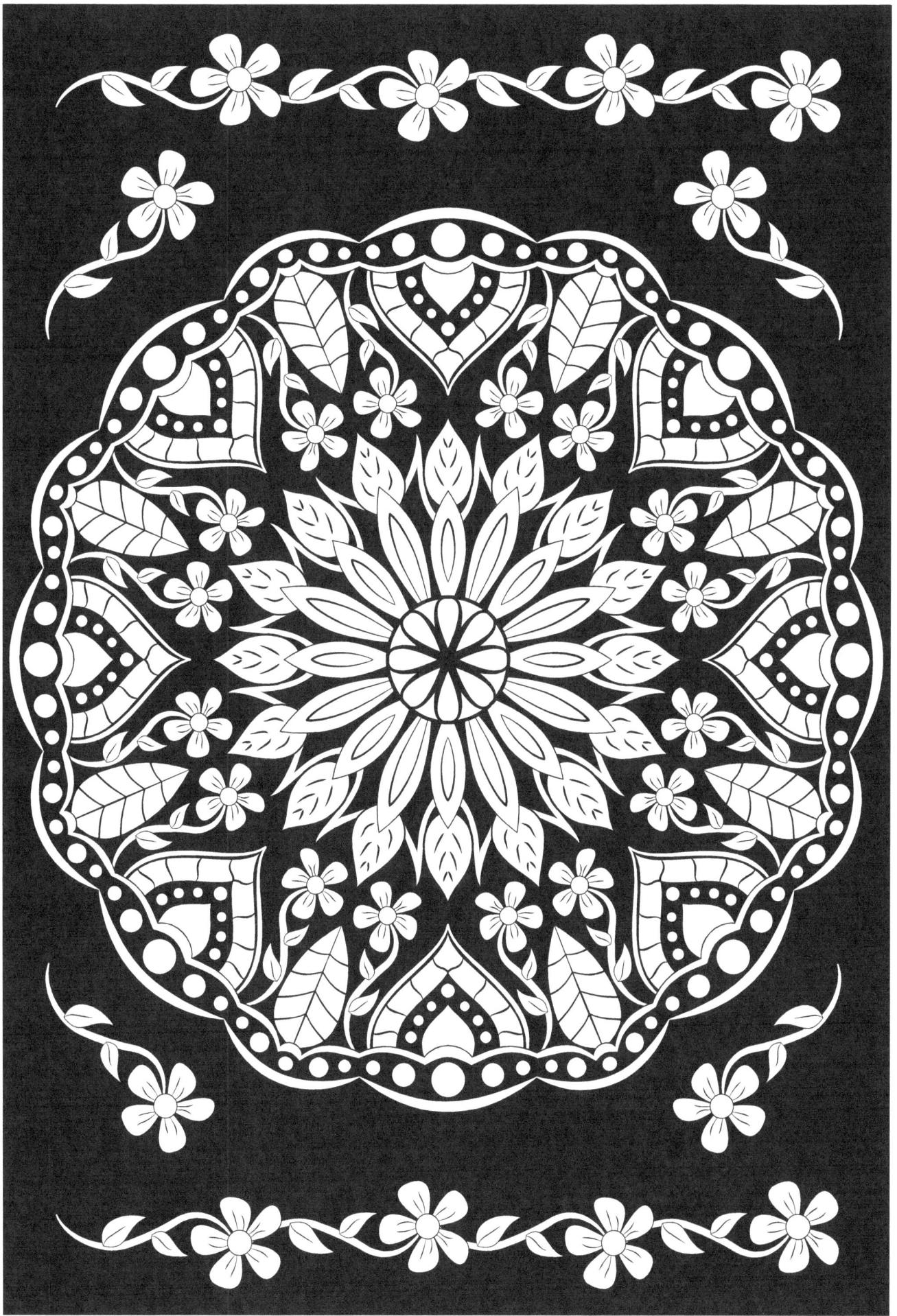

Colored by: _____

OrnaMENTALs™ #0185 "Springtime Splendor"

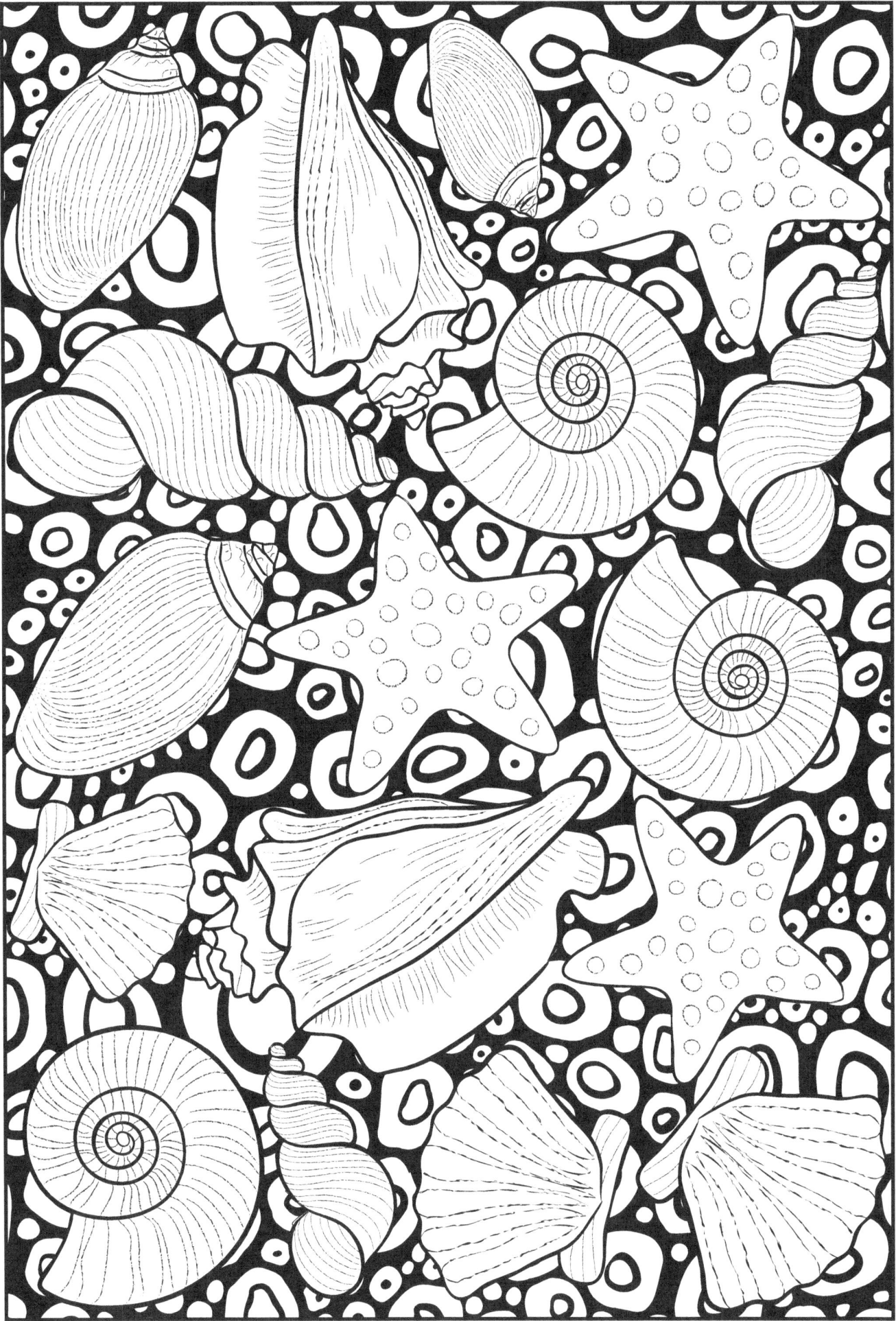

Colored by: _____

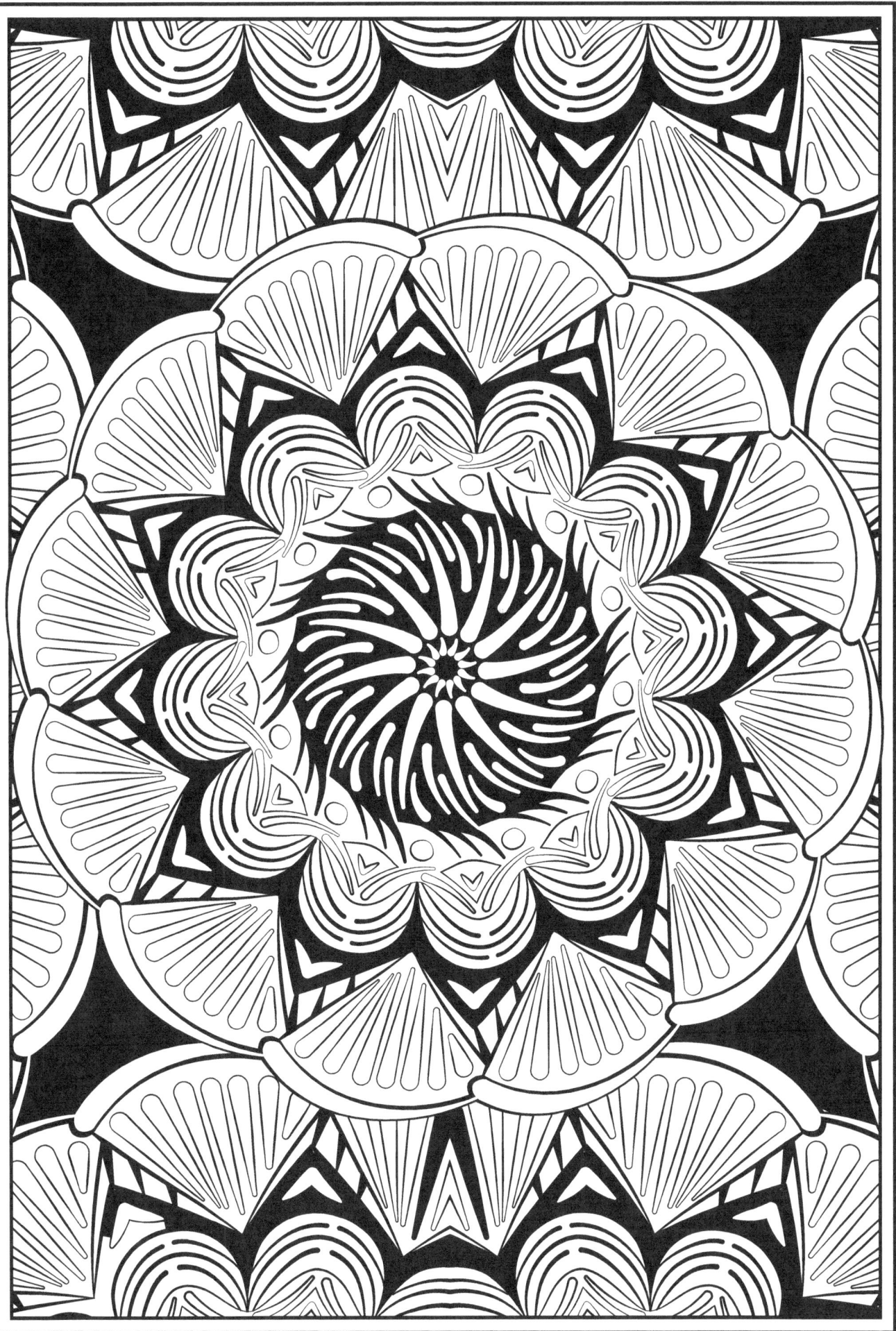

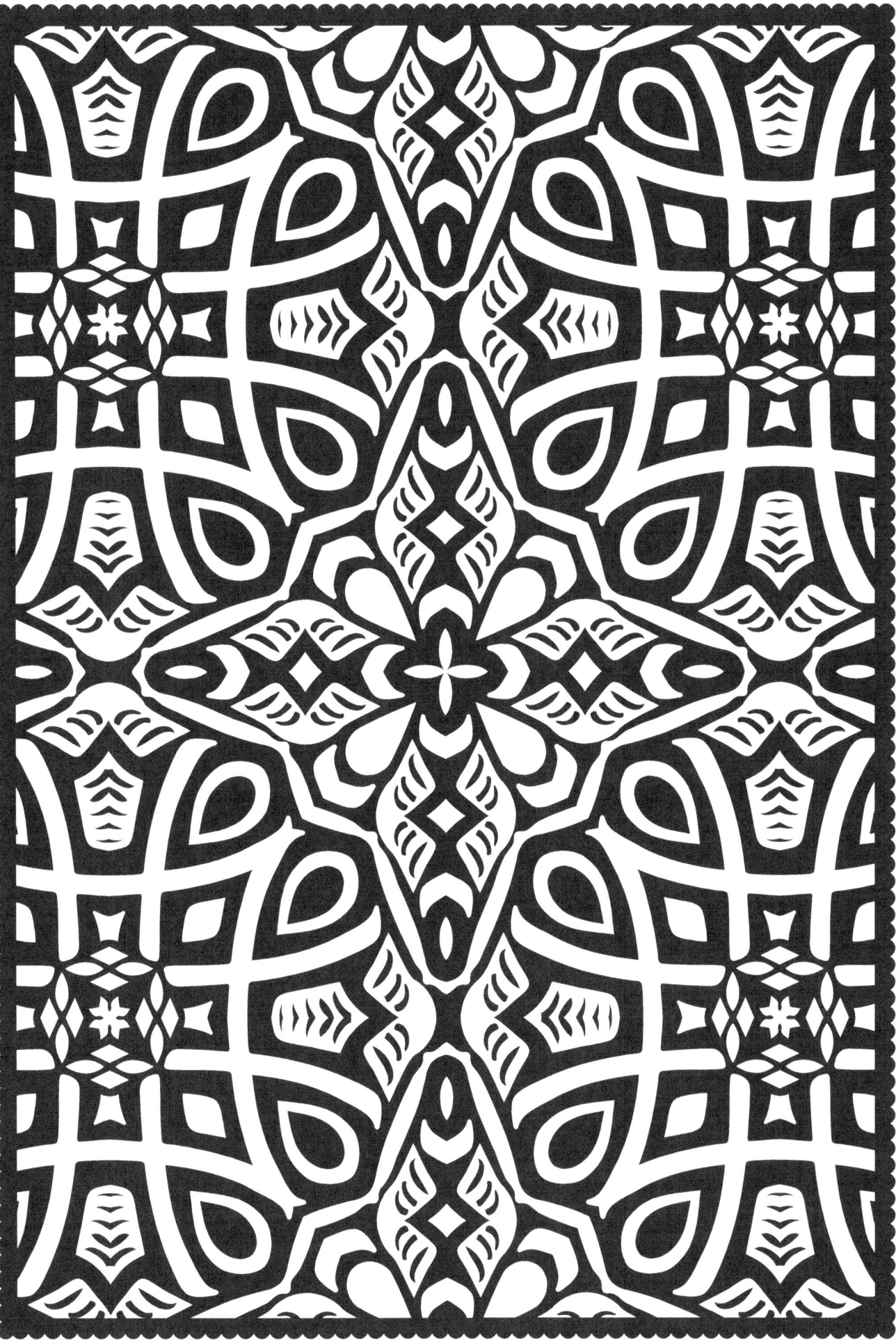

Colored by: _____

Colored by: _____

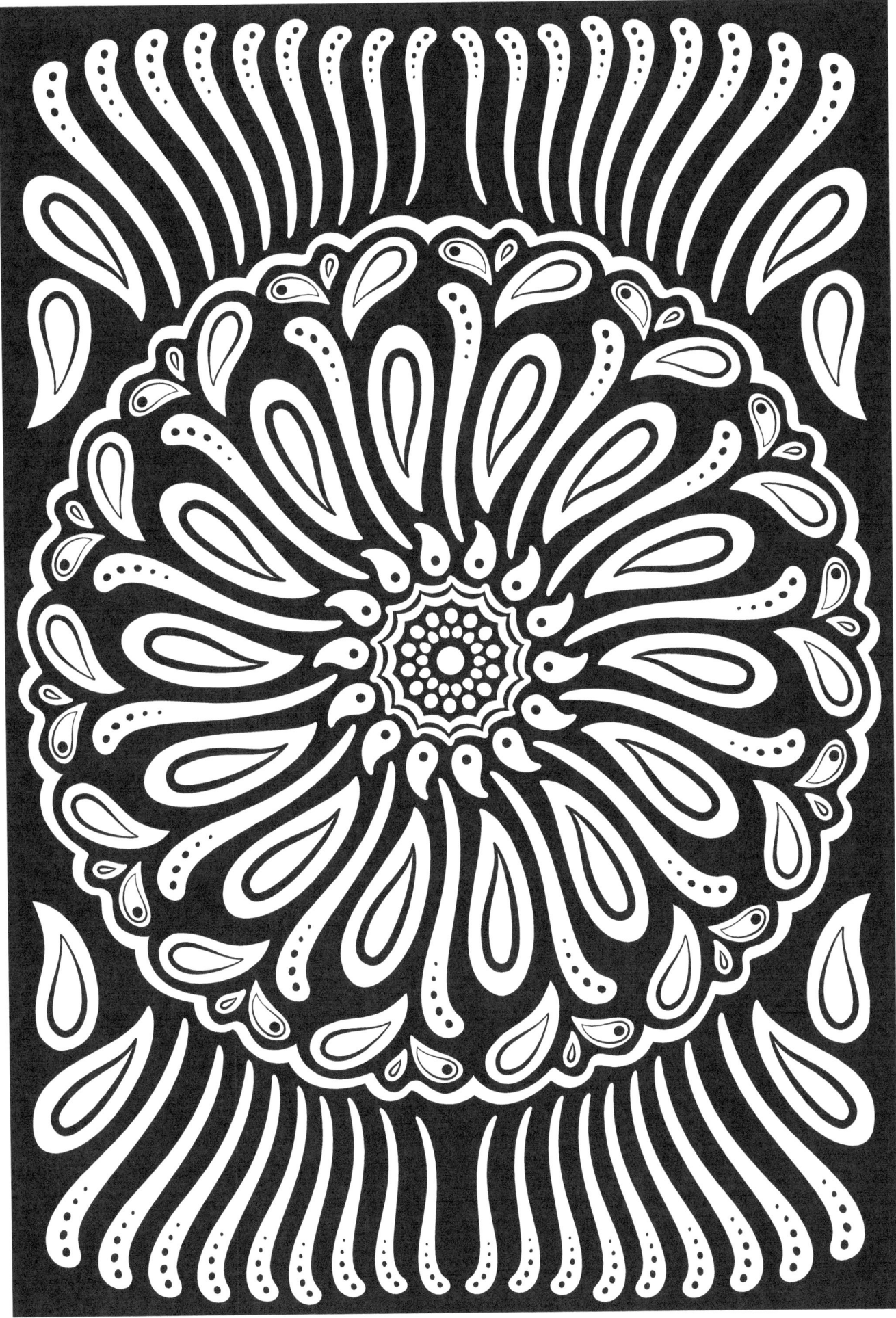

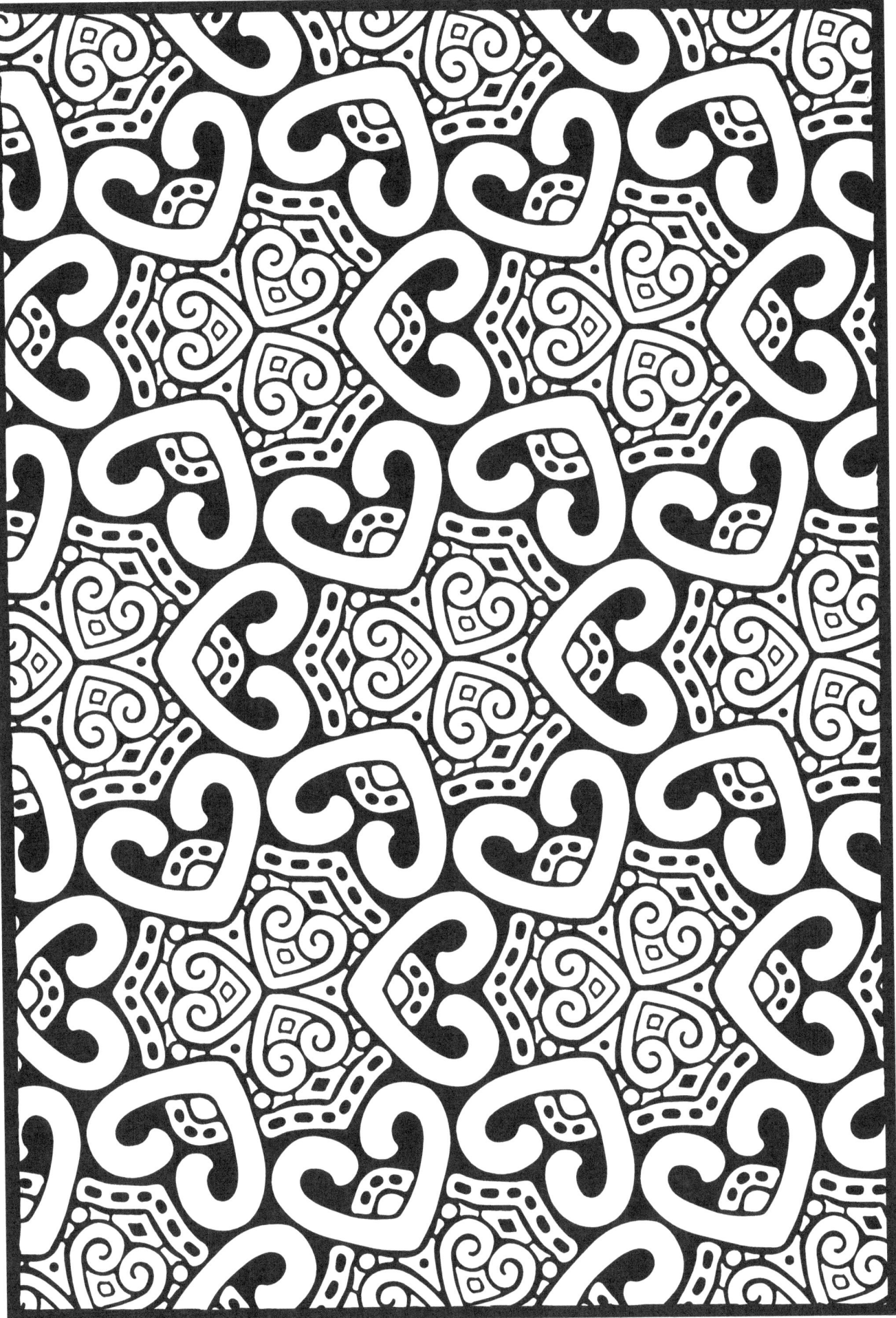

Colored by: _____

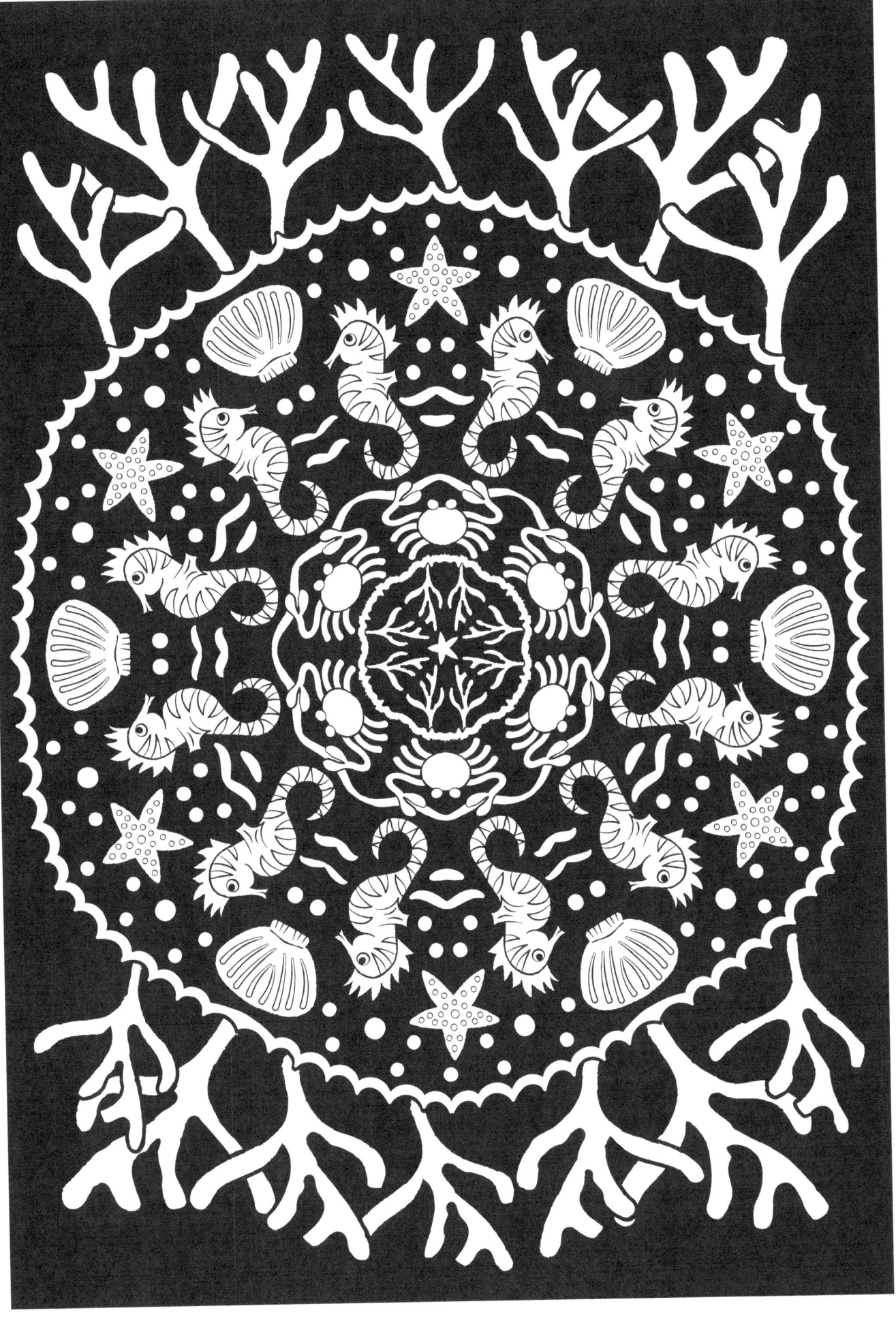

Colored by: _____

Colored by: _____

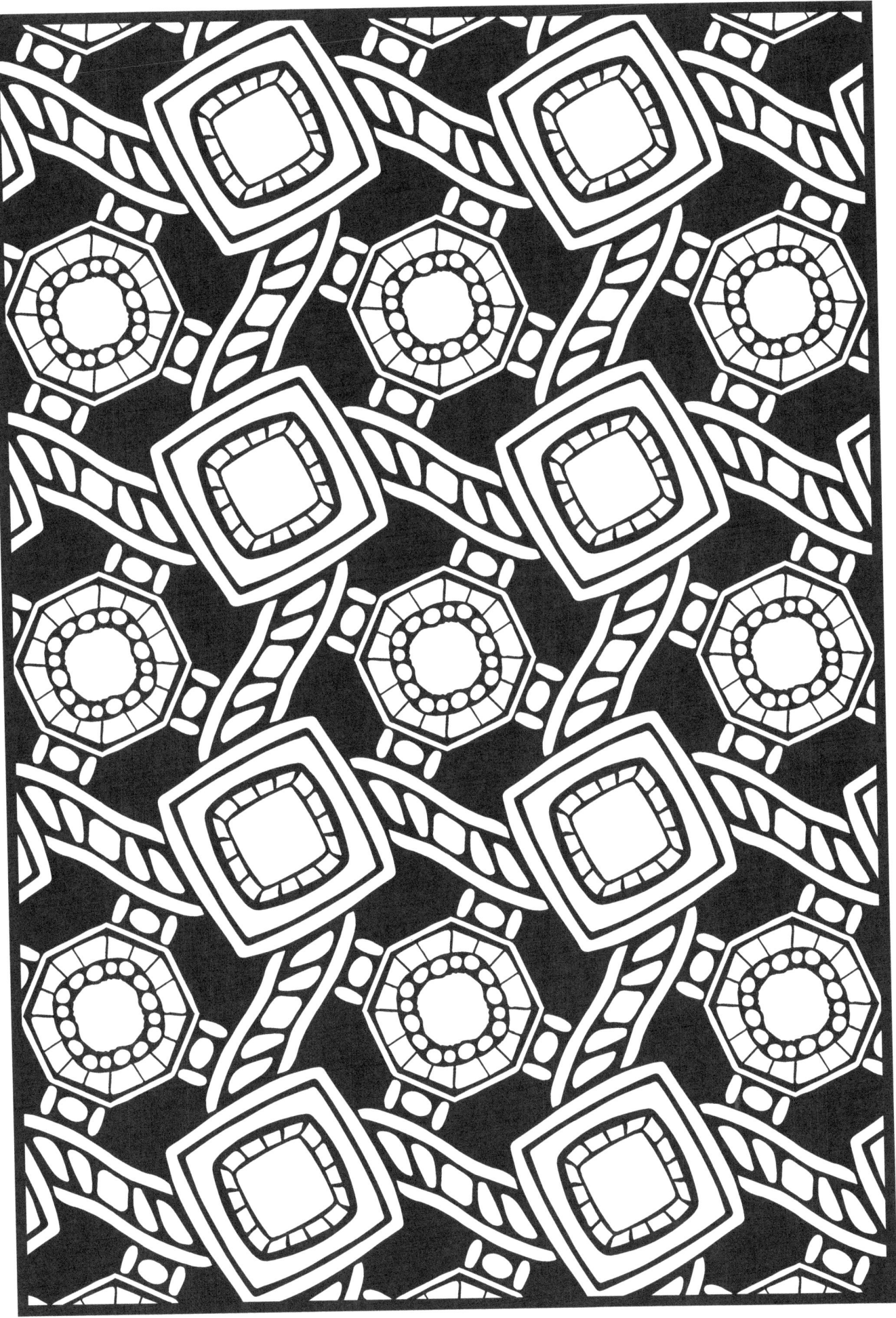

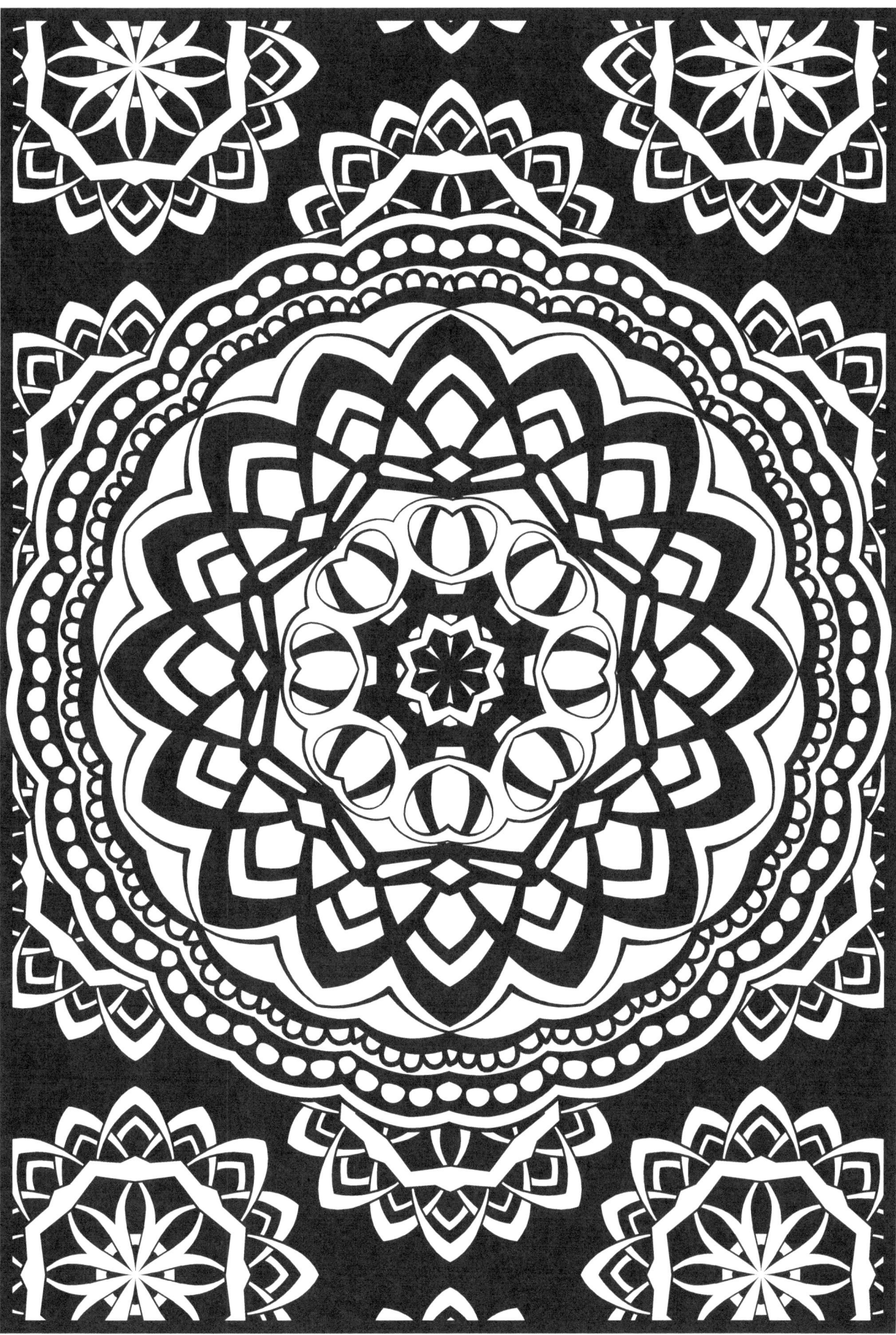

Colored by: _____

Colored by: _____

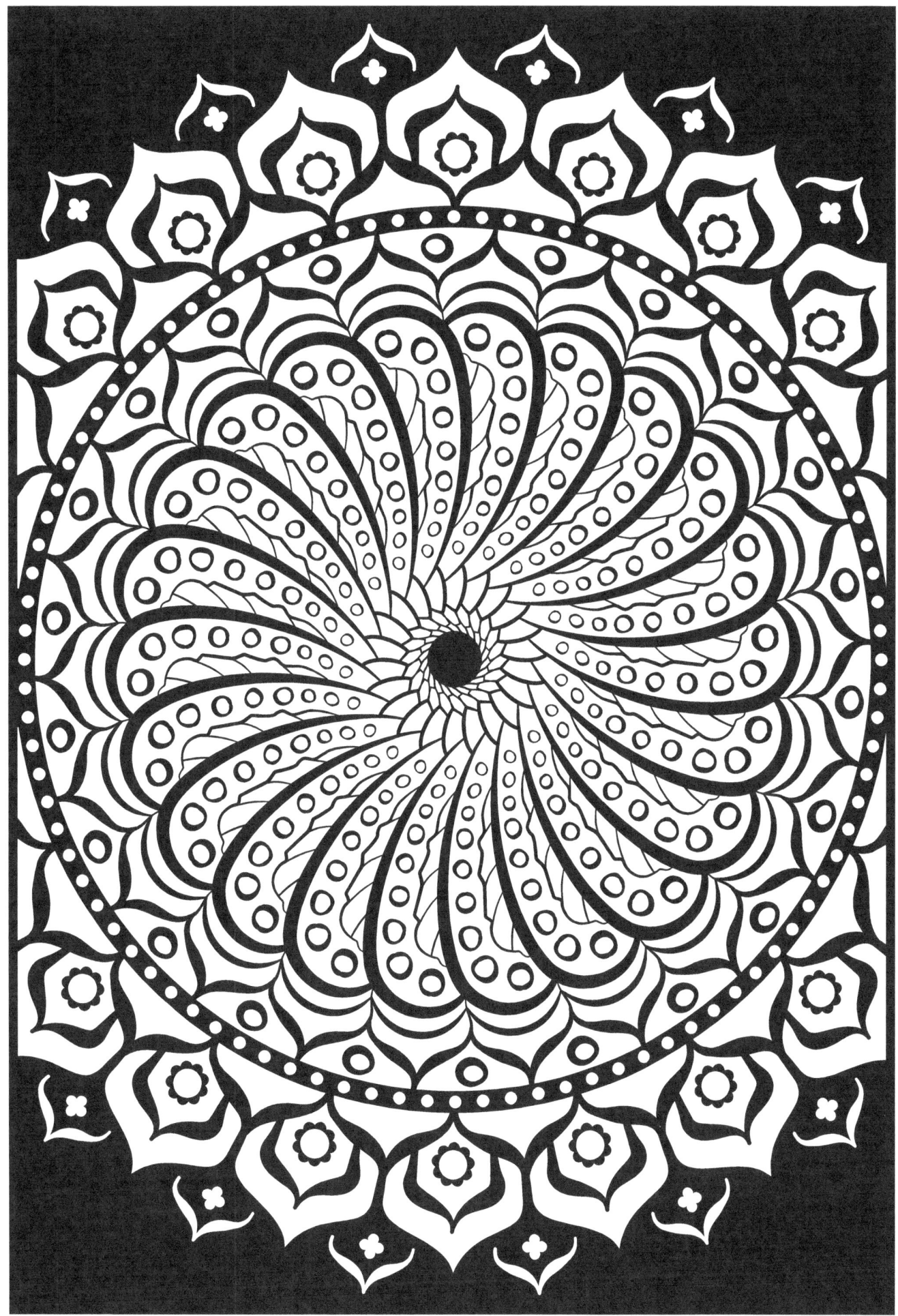

Colored by: _____

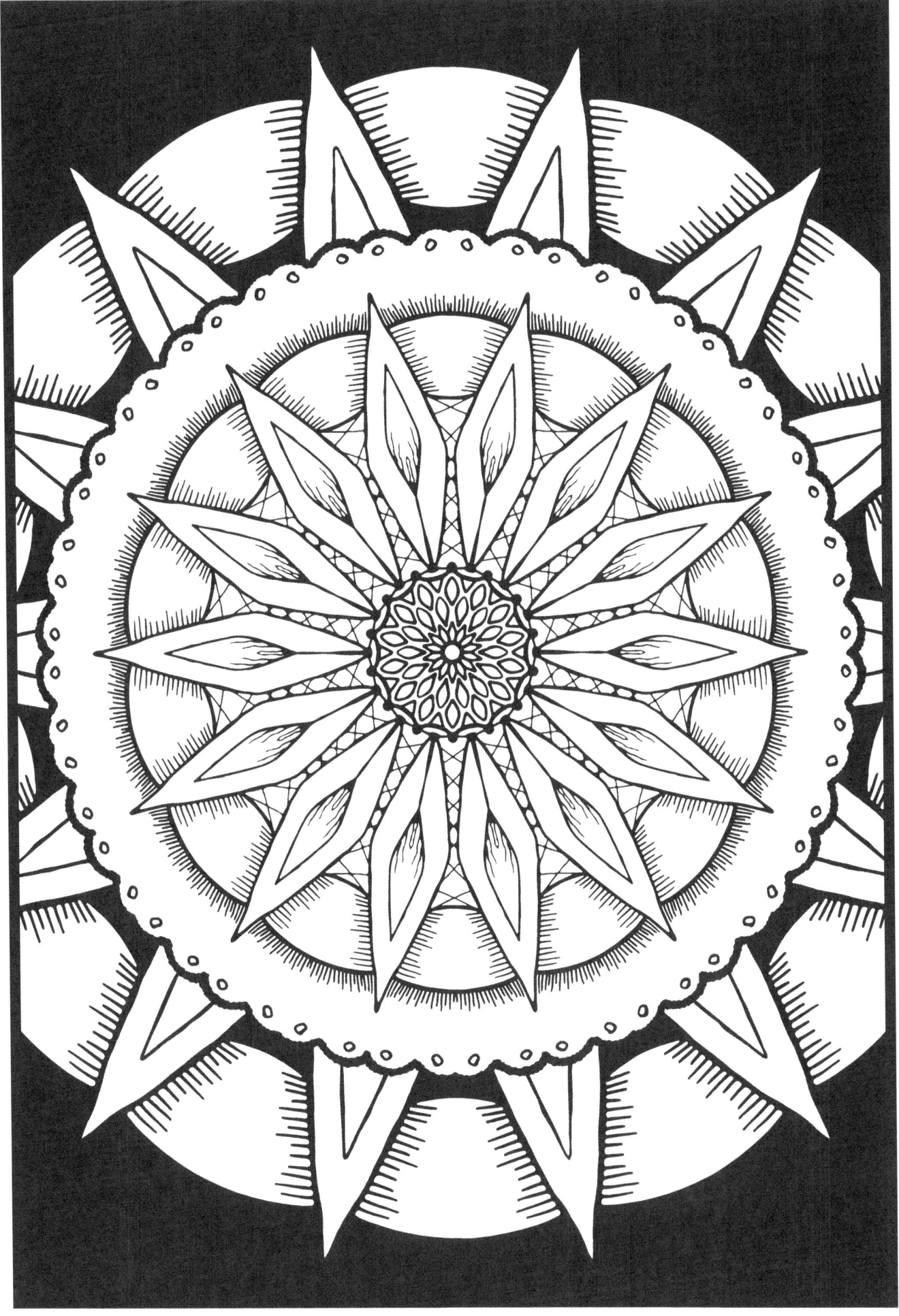

Colored by:

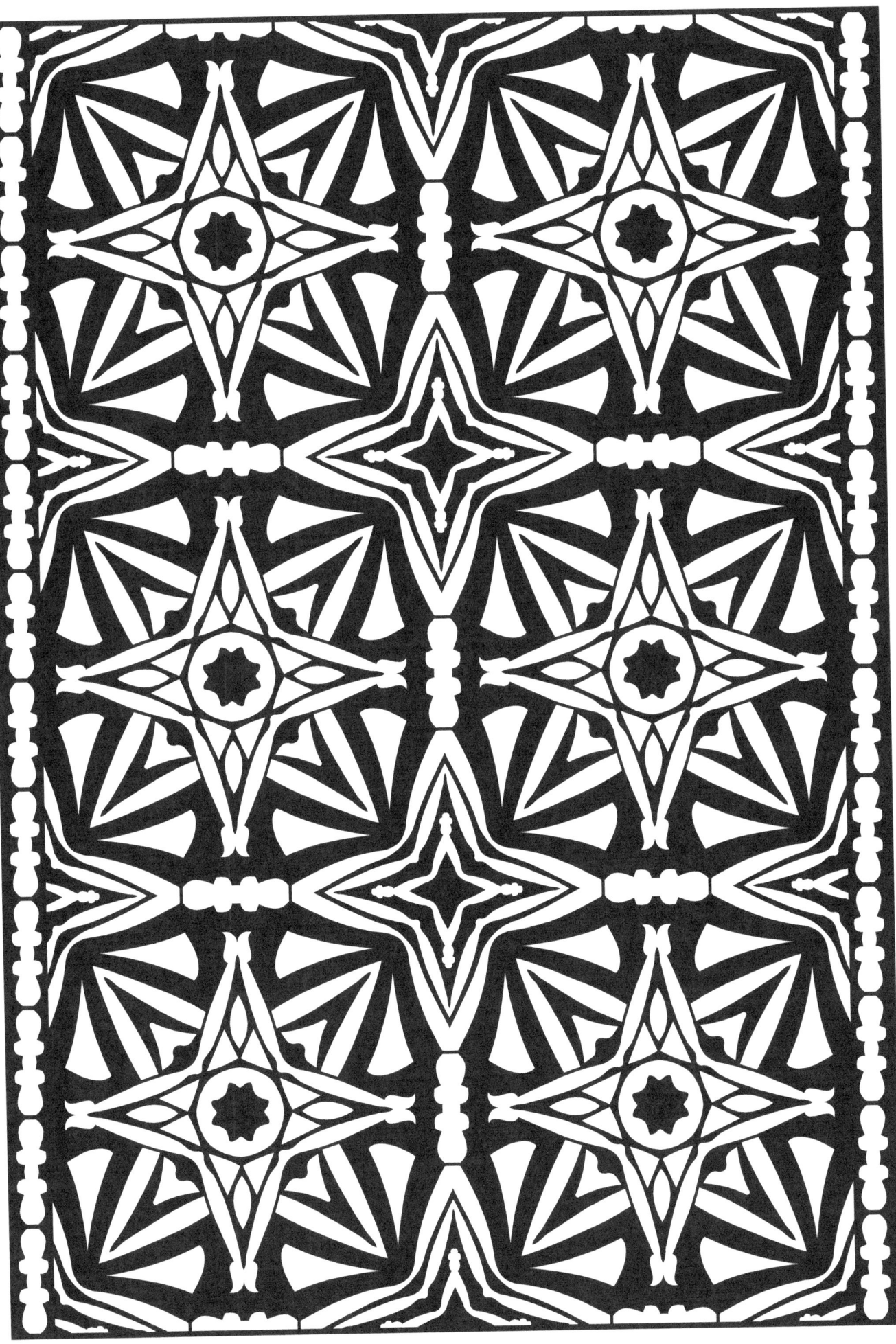

Colored by: _____

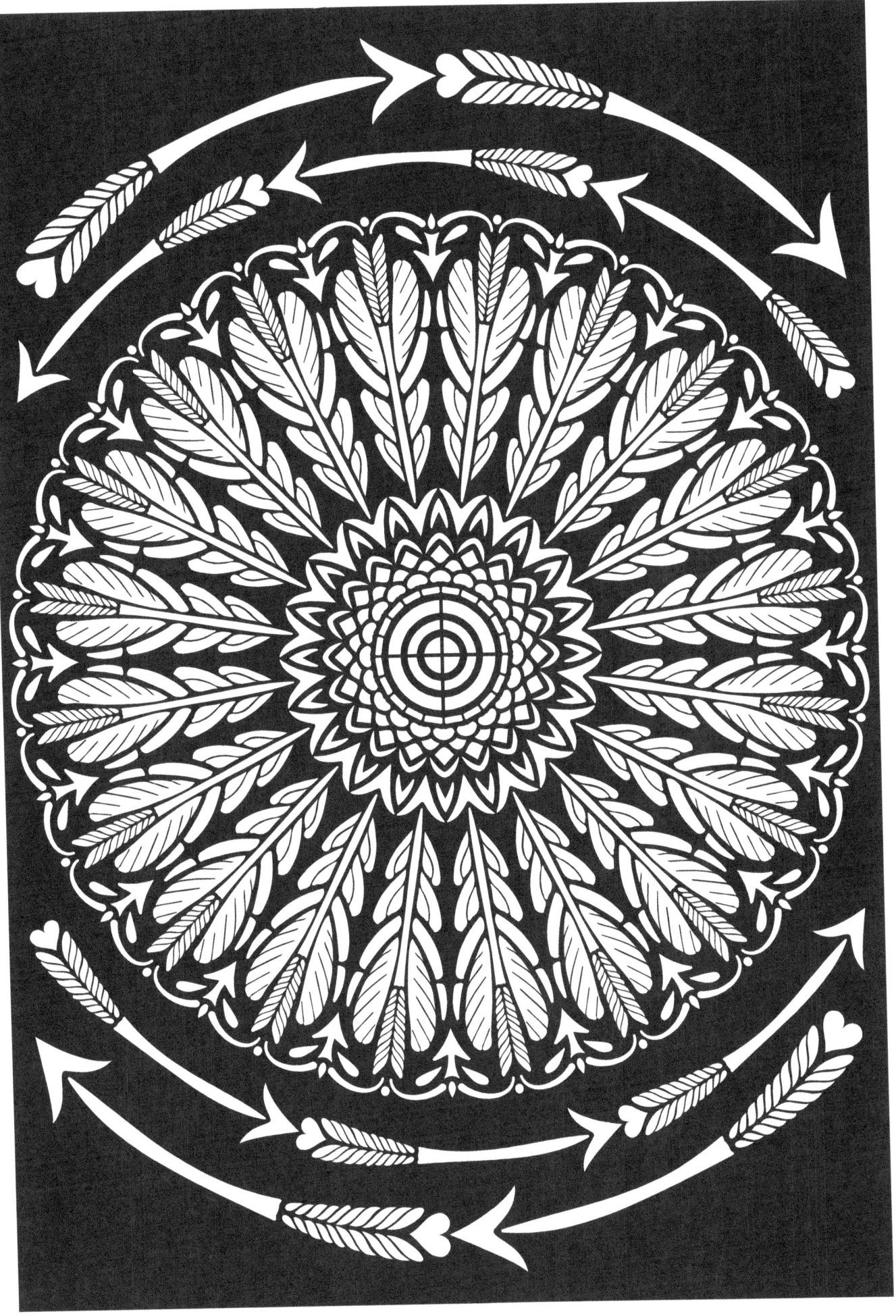

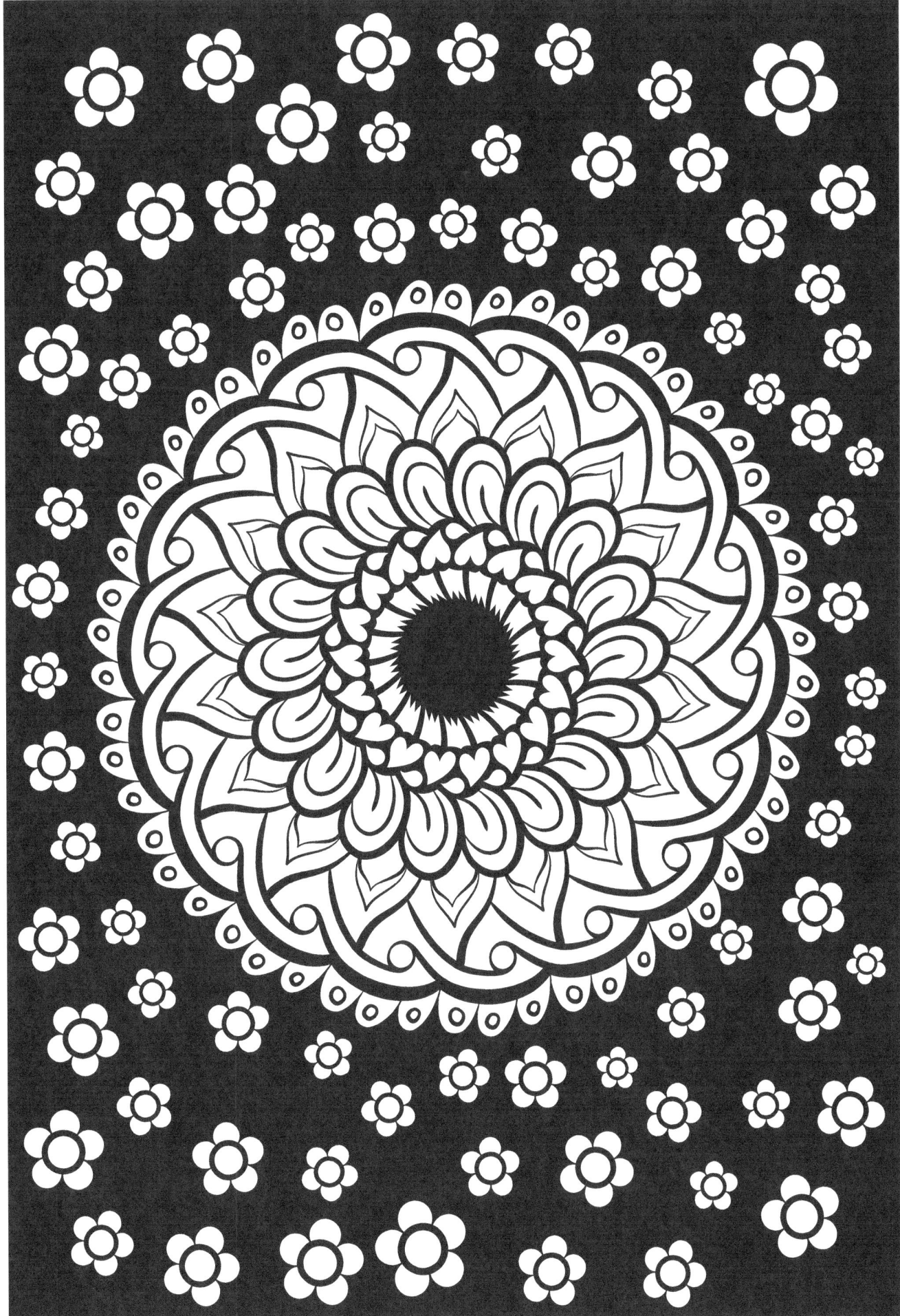

Colored by: _____

OrnaMENTALs™ #0181 "Flower Burst"

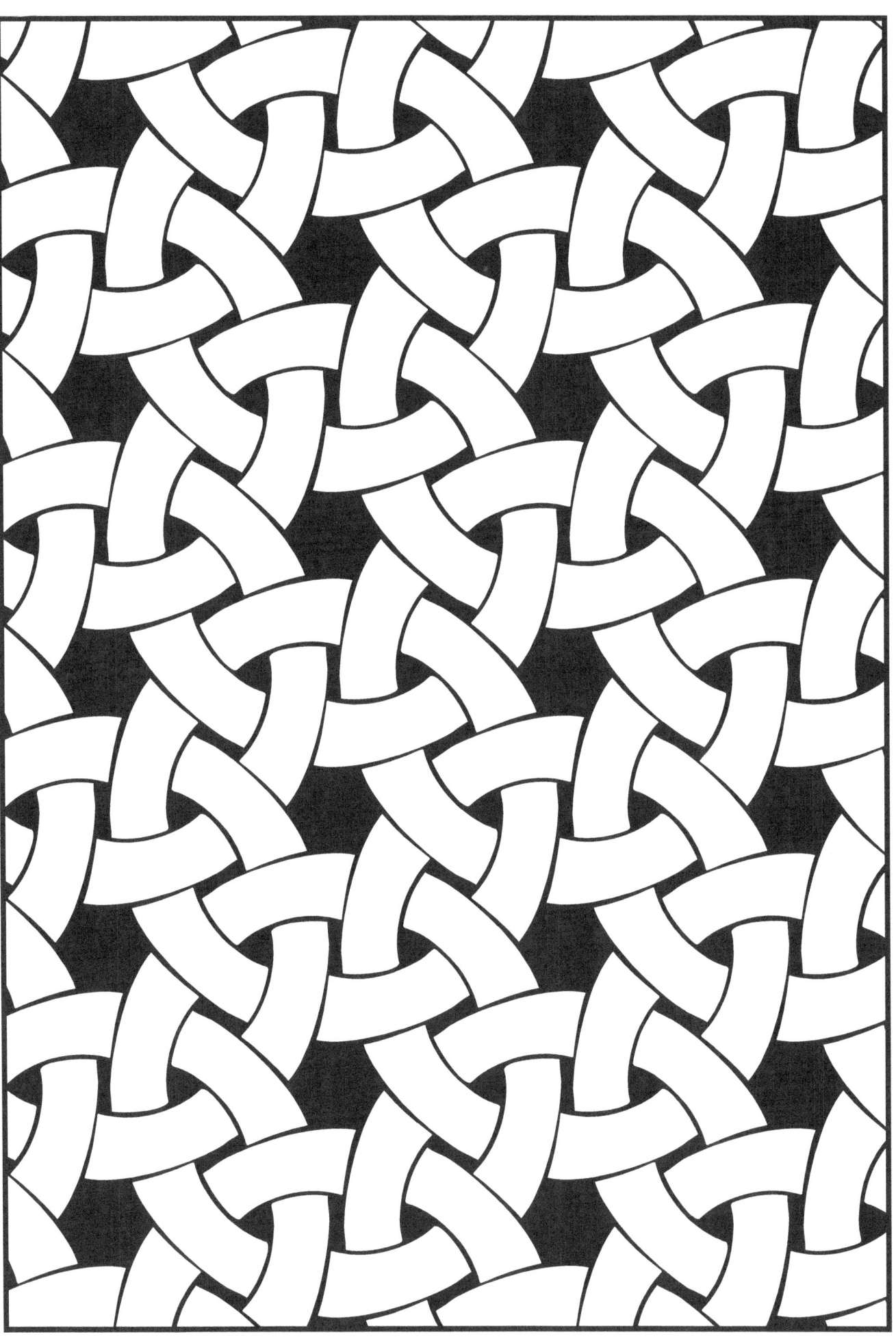

Colored by: _____

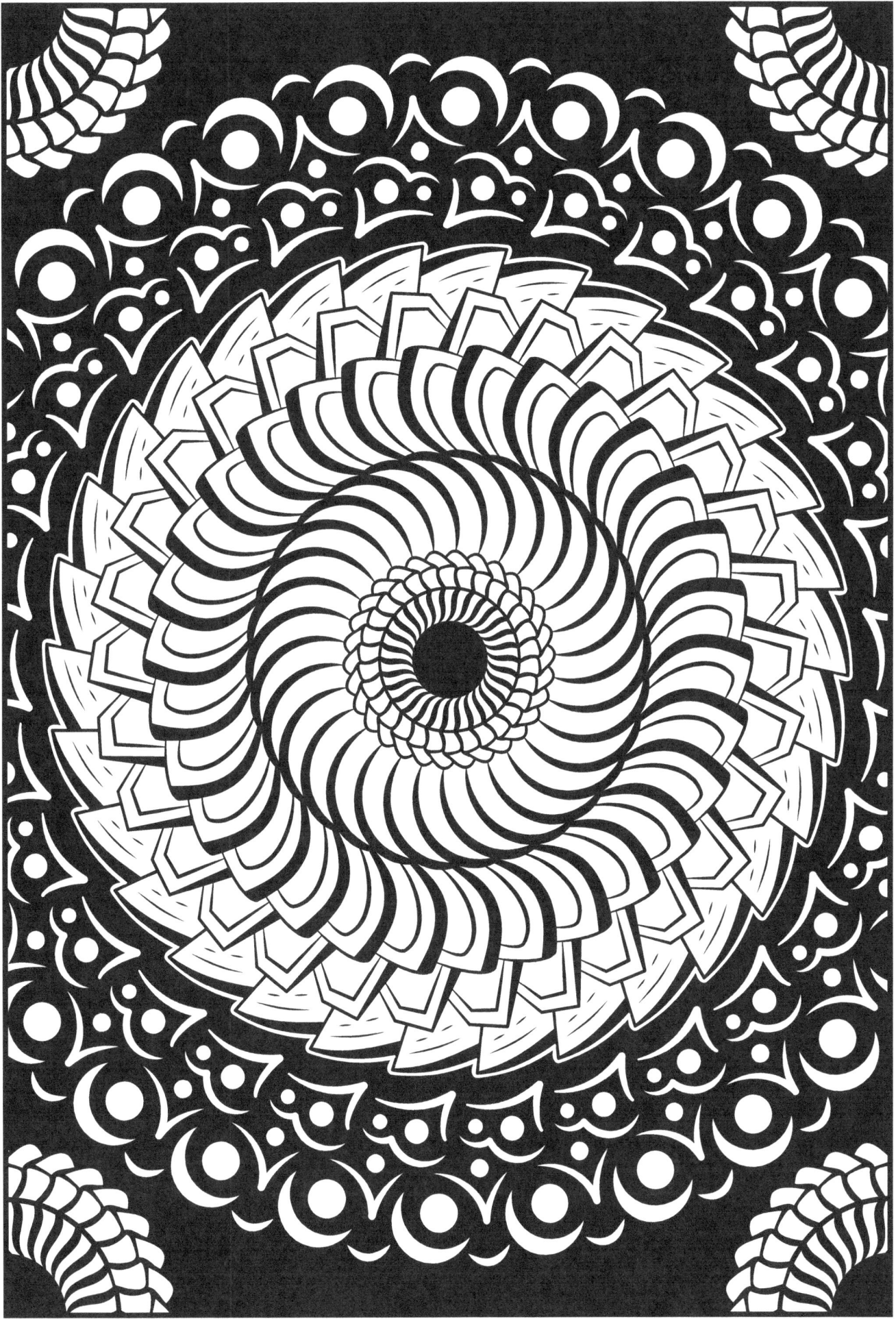

Colored by: _____

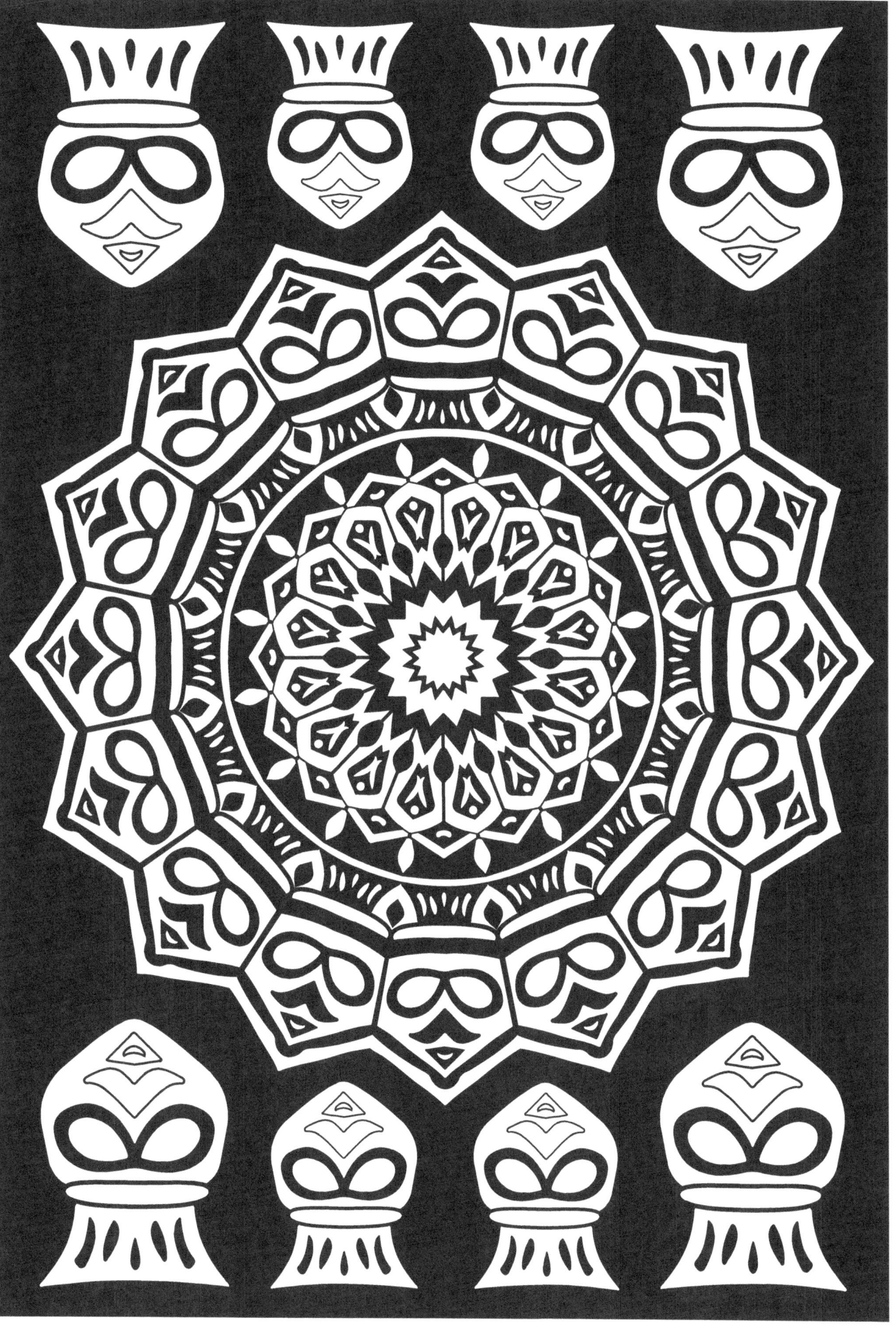

Colored by: _____

BONUS ILLUSTRATIONS

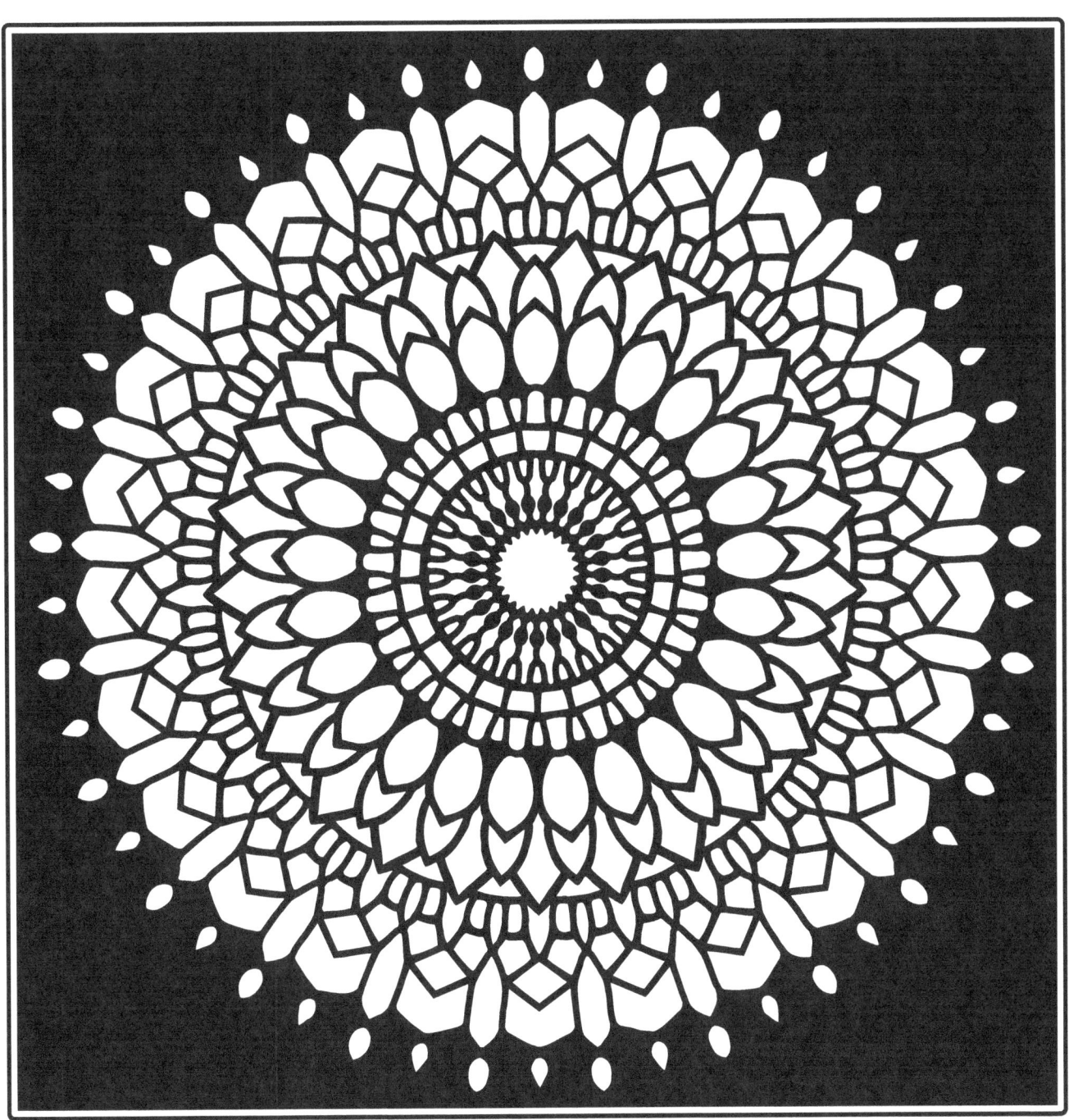

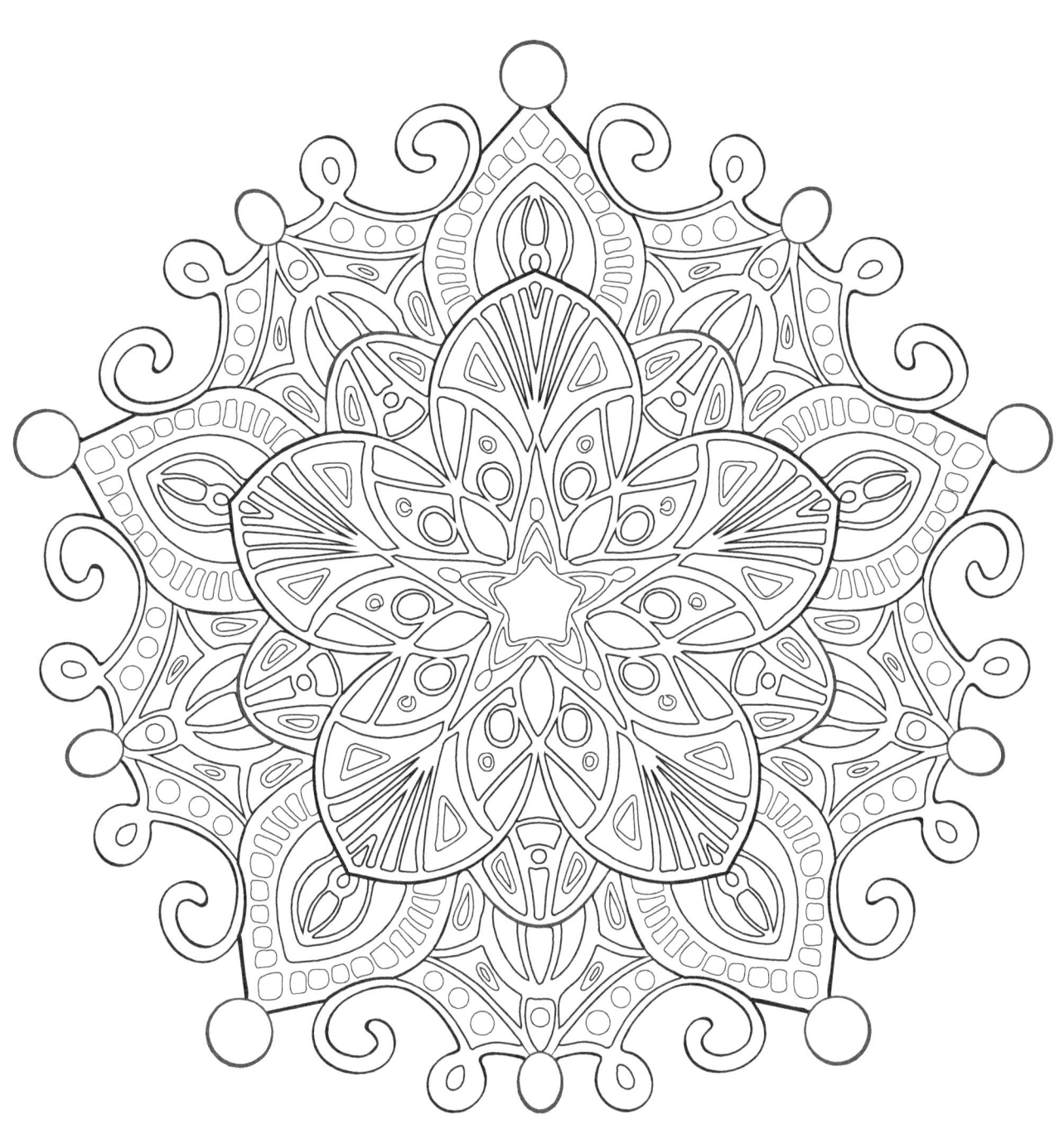

OrnaMENTALs Design #0020 "Majestic Star"
Sample from *OrnaMENTALs Whimsical Mandalas*

© Sue Chastain, suziqcreations.com

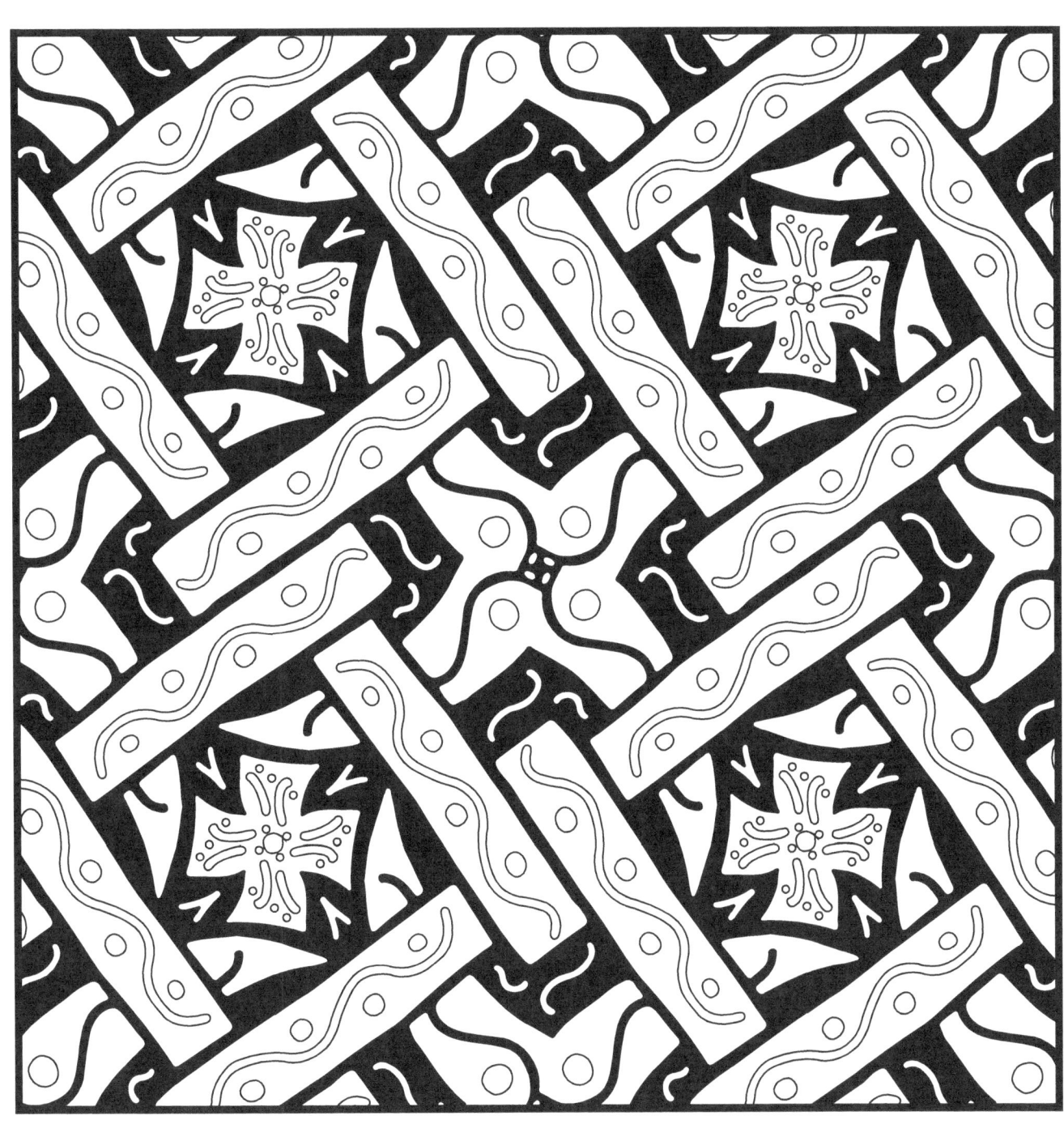

OrnaMENTALs Design #0040 "Cross Pieces"
Sample from *OrnaMENTALs Splendid Symmetry*

© Sue Chastain, suziqcreations.com

OrnaMENTALs Design #0116 "Smile"
Sample from *OrnaMENTALs Feel Good Words Coloring Book*

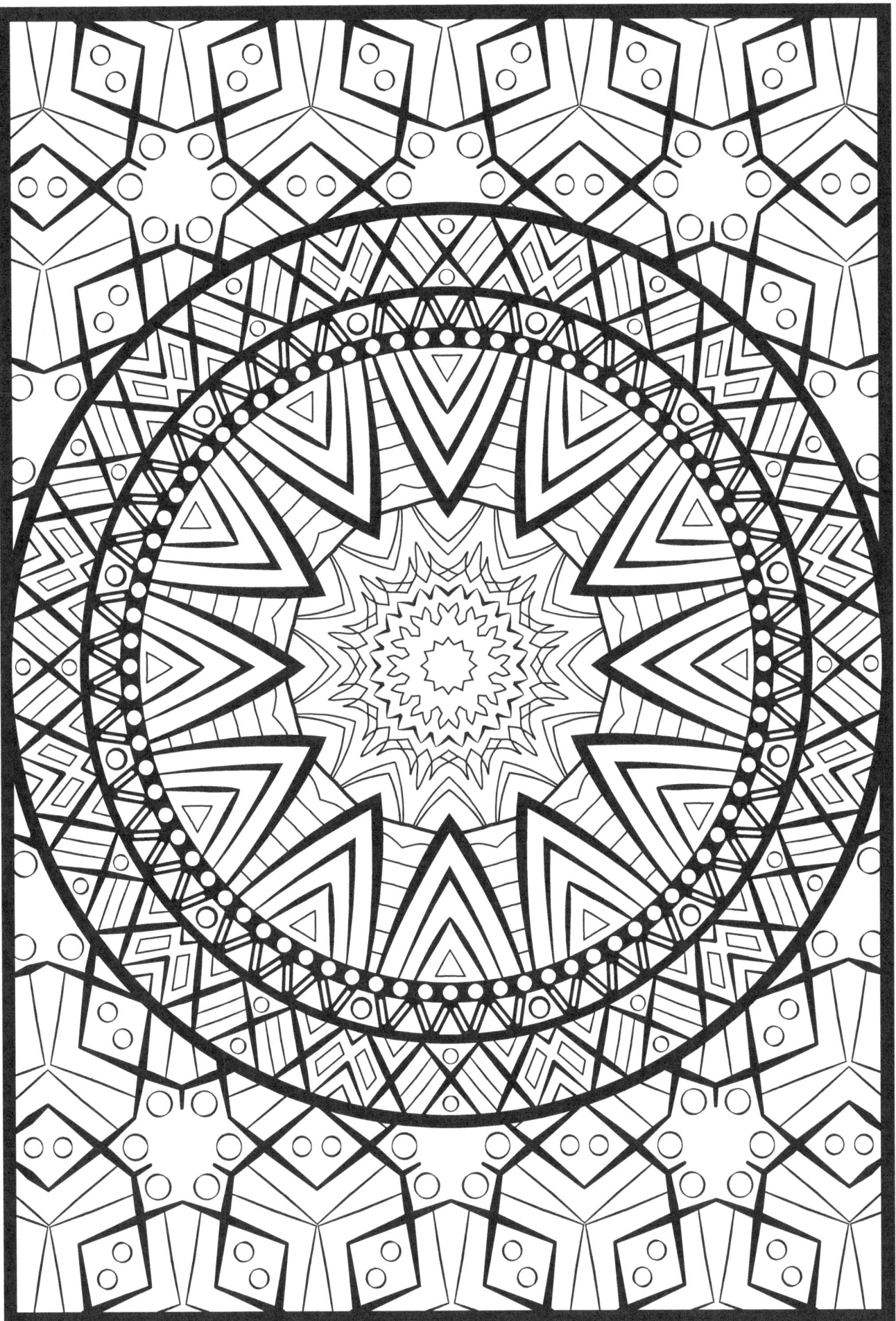

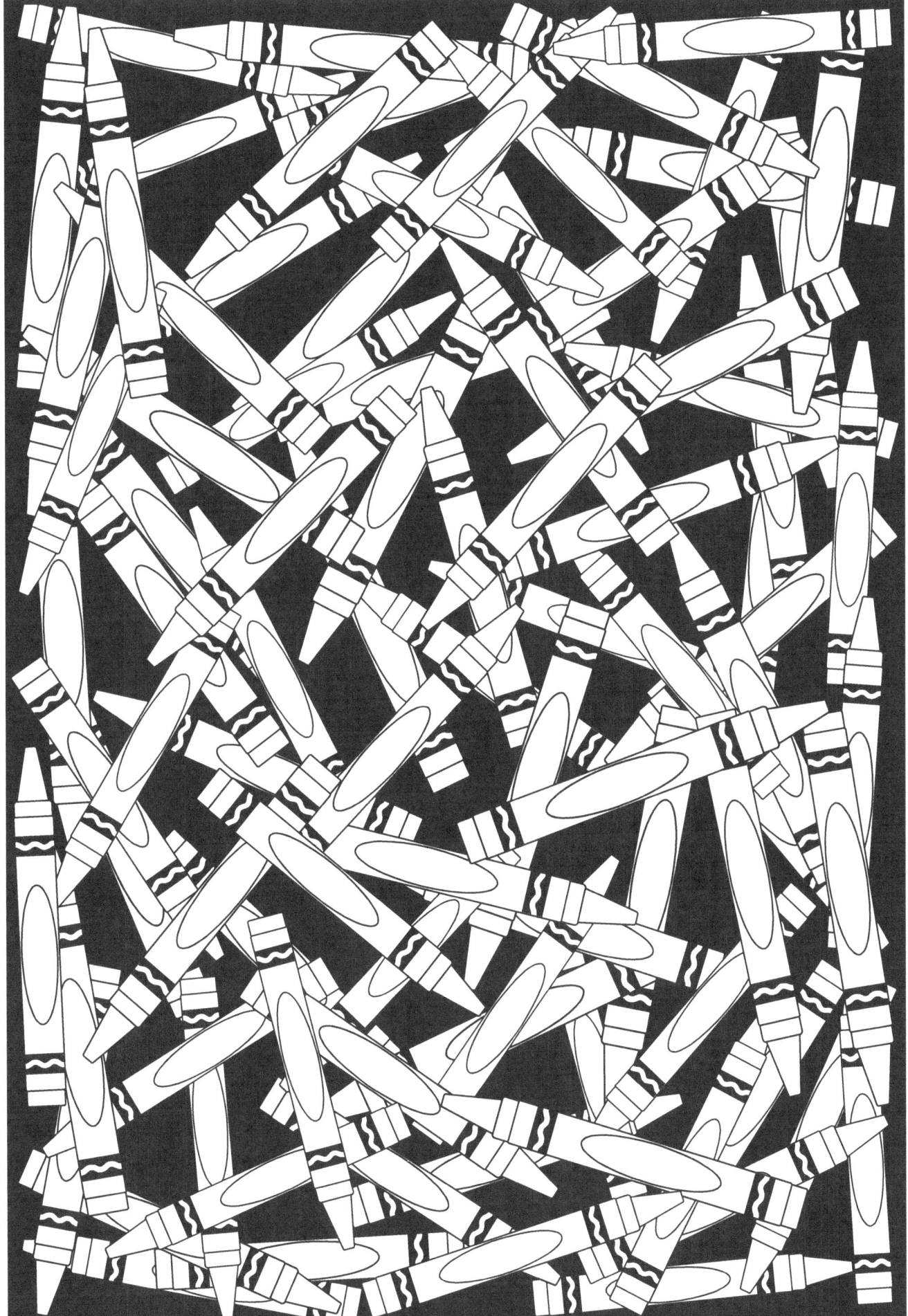

OrnaMENTALs™ #0184 "Brand New Crayons - Ordered"

Bonus! Use this sheet to create a reference chart for your colors, or tear it out to use as a protective blotter page under a page you're coloring.

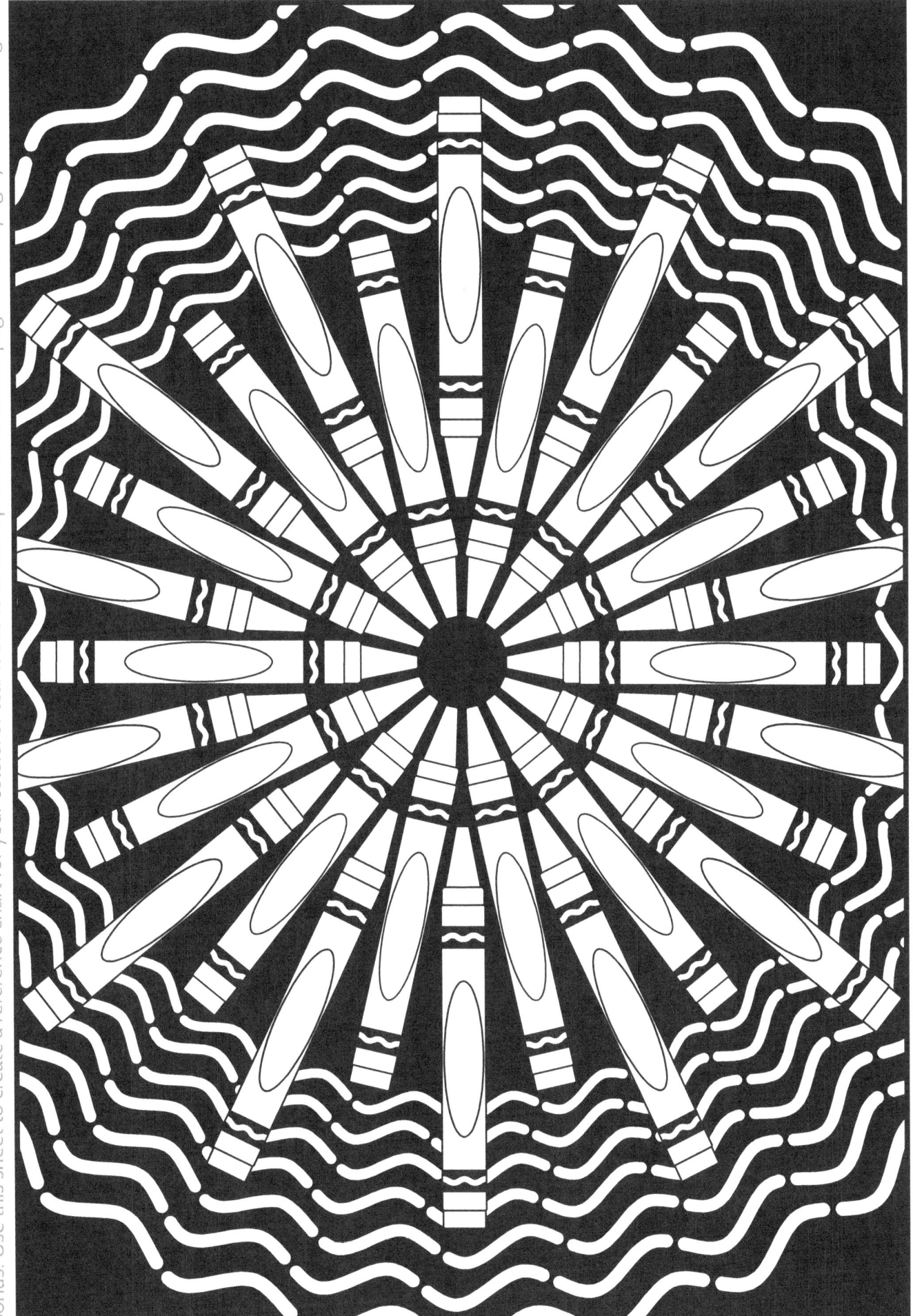

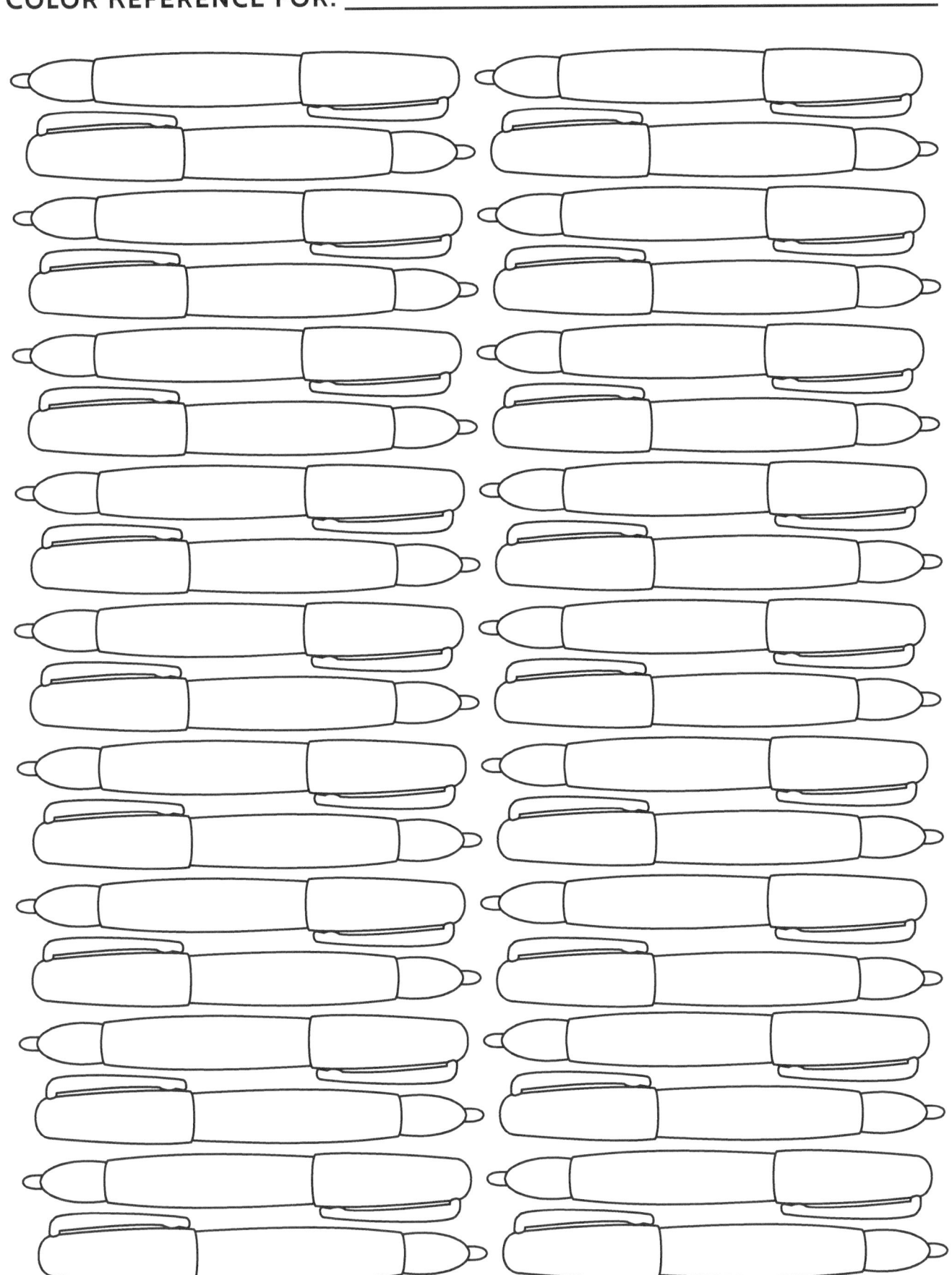

Use this sheet to create a color reference chart for your markers, pens and pencils. or tear it out to use as a protective blotter page under a page you're coloring.

© Sue Chastain. suziqcreations.com

Stay in Touch and Explore More!

I would love to see your talent! Visit suziqcreations.com to show off your coloring. Use the search box to find the book title, then use the comment form to add a picture and a note.

OrnaMENTALs™ Hub on SuziQ Creations (Tips, Samples, and More)
- suziqcreations.com/ornamentals/

Color Schemes for Coloring Inspiration
- suziqcreations.com/colors/

Coloring Craft Ideas, Tutorials, and Tips
- suziqcreations.com/tutorials/

Please contact me for custom designs and special requests.
- suziqcreations.com/contact/

Coloring Books and Digital Downloads

OrnaMENTALs Feel Good Words To-Go
- suziqcreations.com/feelgood-portable/

OrnaMENTALs Feel Good Words
- suziqcreations.com/feelgood/

MiniMENTALs On-the-Go Coloring Book
- suziqcreations.com/mini/

OrnaMENTALs Splendid Symmetry
- suziqcreations.com/splendid/

OrnaMENTALs Whimsical Mandalas
- suziqcreations.com/whimsical/

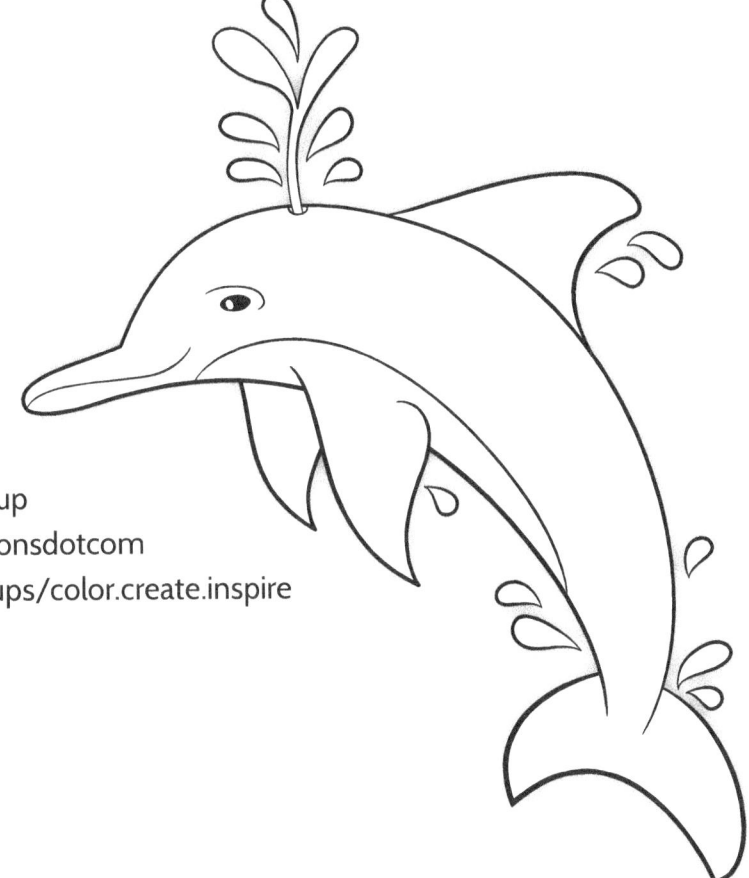

Follow SuziQ Creations:
- **Sue's News:** suziqcreations.com/signup
- **Facebook:** facebook.com/suziqcreationsdotcom
- **Facebook Group:** facebook.com/groups/color.create.inspire
- **Pinterest:** pinterest.com/mesue1/
- **Twitter:** @suechastain
- **Instagram:** @suechastain
- **Google Plus:** +SueChastain
- **Tumblr:** suechastain.tumblr.com

♡ **If you enjoyed this book, please add a review on Amazon:** suziqcreations.com/lor